Thirsting for God

by

Ralph I. Tilley

As the deer pants for the water brooks,

So my soul pants for You, O God.

My soul thirsts for God, for the living God . . .

— Psalm 42:1-2a, NASB

Thirsting for God

by

Ralph I. Tilley

LITS Books
P.O. Box 405
Sellersburg, Indiana, 47172

Published by LITS Books
A ministry of Life in the Spirit Ministries, Inc.
P.O. Box 405
Sellersburg, Indiana 47172
www.litsjournal.org

ISBN 978-0-615-48529-4

To three lovely ladies—
Emily,
my love and inspiration
in every venture of consequence,
Rochelle Lyn and Julie Kae,
our daughters
who continue to shower us with immeasurable joy—
this volume is affectionately dedicated.

Contents

Preface

The title and theme of this volume—*Thirsting for God*—has been the undercurrent of my soul since the Lord Jesus mercifully entered my life as a teenager. That thirst for God, while ebbing and flowing through the years, has always been present. With the sweet singer of Israel, my dominant cry has repeatedly been, "As the deer pants for the water brooks, so my soul pants for You, O God. My soul thirsts for God, for the living God ..." (Psalm 42:1-2a, NASB).

Thirsting for God is a compilation of poetry, mediations, and prayers—writings which I believe project an honest expression of my own aspirations, regrets and disappointments, confessions and doubts, praises and gratitude, as well as some observations about how as Christians we are called by God to live in this world. These writings are imperfect, to be sure, but hopefully our Lord will be pleased to use them to stir up a few of his children to thirst for a deeper intimacy with Christ and a more fruitful Christian life.

When I was editing this material for publication, I discovered that a recurring theme in this volume is *change*. I suspect this is a prominent theme in my writings because of the changes our gracious Lord made in my life soon after my conversion event, as well as the ongoing changes he continues to perform. And I further suspect that the theme is as pronounced as it is because I believe today's church is seeing far too little visible change in the lives of her "converts." I am of the conviction that Jesus always makes a difference when he shows up—in one life, or in one church.

It was not until I was in the fifth decade of my life that I began to write seriously, having discerned that it may please the Lord for me to begin to put some of my thoughts down on paper. Thus, a little church bulletin insert became the forerunner of what is now *Life in the Spirit* journal. Some years later, following a disappointing ministry experience, I began to write poetry. This endeavor has brought me immeasurable satisfaction as I've worked to put into verse form what my *eyes* have seen and my *ears* have heard. Furthermore, the Lord has often used the writing of prayers over the years to help me to better express in words of praise, thanksgiving, confession, and intercession, what was going on in my heart.

The contents of this volume, for the most part, first appeared in *Life in the Spirit* journal. I also included two family-related poems: one relating to my grandson Luke; the other written by my mother. Generally, each meditation following a poem addresses the same subject. However, where there is no meditation following a poem, I have included "The Speaking Word" feature, which provides a biblical perspective on the previous poem.

With gratitude for the editorial assistance of Frances Moore, Philip Estes, my daughter Rochelle Farah, and my wife Emily, I now send forth *Thirsting for God* to the Christian reading public with a petition, a confession, and an aspiration, shaped by the words of three of our Lord's choice saints.

Amy Carmichael (1867-1951):

Take this book in Thy wounded Hand,
Jesus, Lord of Calvary,
Let it go forth at Thy command,
Use it as it pleaseth Thee.

Robert Murray M'Cheyne (1813-1843):

"I fear I shall never be in this world what I desire."

Thomas O. Chisholm (1866-1960):

I have one deep, supreme desire,
That I may be like Jesus.
To this I fervently aspire,
That I may be like Jesus.

Now, dear reader, may the gracious Holy Spirit be pleased to use these devotional writings to create in you an insatiable thirst for the one and only true God and Father of our Lord Jesus Christ.

Soli Deo Gloria!

God of All Creation

God of all creation,
with grateful hearts we raise
Ceaseless adoration
from dawn's earliest rays.

Lord of all universe,
we bow to your control;
Turning from our own ways,
your sovereignty extol.

Father of all offspring,
we lift your name highly,
And as one fam'ly sing,
"Holy, holy, holy."

Savior of humankind,
our hearts are filled with praise;
Alone in you we find
salvation all our days.

Spirit of fire and pow'r,
descend anew we pray;
That from this sacred hour,
our hearts may never stray.

The Speaking Word

God of all creation . . .

[1]The heavens declare the glory of God, and the sky above proclaims his handiwork. [2]Day to day pours out speech, and night to night reveals knowledge.

— Psalm 19:1-2

Lord of all universe . . .

By faith we understand that the universe was created by the word of God, so that what is seen was not made out of things that are visible.

— Hebrews 11:6

Father of all offspring . . .

See what kind of love the Father has given to us, that we should be called children of God; and so we are.

— 1 John 3:1

Savior of humankind . . .

[4]But when the goodness and loving kindness of God our Savior appeared, [5]he saved us, not because of works done by us in righteousness, but according to his own mercy, by the washing of regeneration and renewal of the Holy Spirit . . .

— Titus 3:4-5

Spirit of fire and pow'r . . .

"I baptize you with water for repentance, but he who is coming after me is mightier than I, whose sandals I am not worthy to carry. He will baptize you with the Holy Spirit and Fire."

— Matthew 3:11

Prayer of Thanksgiving to God the Father

It was your Spirit who first whispered the word in my heart many years ago: "Father." I once knew you as God, but that night I came to know you as my Father in Heaven.

What wonder, how amazing—the mystery and ineffable glory which surround you on your eternal throne. And yet . . . you mercifully chose to reveal yourself to man through your unique Son, the Lord Jesus Christ. Your Son said of those who had seen him, that they also had seen the Father.

I praise and thank you, O my Father, for the perfections of your Person. Everywhere I look in this world I see the stark reality of the results of the Fall. Nothing here is perfect. The best achievements of humankind are miserably flawed. But you, holy Father, are perfect. No defects exist in your Person. You are complete and whole in yourself. You lack nothing. You are God. You are God my Father.

I praise and thank you, O my Father, for your love. Were you not a God of perfect love, you would not have created the cosmos; you would not have planned for man's redemption; you would not have given your Son to die as the atoning, vicarious sacrifice for man's salvation; you would not have sent your Spirit to indwell your people; you would not have forgiven me of all my sins; you would not presently be preparing for the

Bride's future inheritance and glory. You are the Father of perfect love.

I praise and thank you, O my Father, for your faithfulness. You are a covenant-keeping Father. There is not one word you have spoken but what will come to pass. Your promises have been guaranteed through the death and resurrection of your Son. Even if heaven and earth should pass away, your Word is eternal, sure and steadfast. You are faithful.

I praise and thank you, O my Father, for your fellowship. That you would give your Son to die, that you would send your very own Spirit to inhabit my body—your temple—that I might commune with you, walk with you, share with you—is more than I can comprehend. Oh, what blessed sweet fellowship! All because you, O Father, planned it all.

I praise and thank you, O my Father, for sealing me with your Holy Spirit. I am no longer under the control of the Enemy. Nor am I any longer my own. The very moment I looked up and trusted your Son as my Savior and Lord, you sent your Holy Spirit to imprint me as your very own child . . . forever. I am yours; you are mine. I am content . . . and still I thirst.

Abba! Father! Amen.

The Son

Inheritor of Father's wealth,
deserving all he owns;
Creator of the universe,
designing vast unknowns.

Reflector of God's pure glory,
deflecting praise to him;
Imprimatur of his Being,
appearing as a man.

Sustainer of all creation,
giving life by his word;
Cleanser of sin and defilement,
atoning by his blood.

Perfecter of our salvation,
overcoming all his foes;
Intercessor for his brothers,
giving hope in our woes.

Superior to winged spirits,
having a greater name;
Wonder of heavenly beings,
exulting in his fame.

Lover of divine righteousness,
clinging to what is good;
Hater of Satan's wickedness,
despising all that's bad.

He is the Father's Beloved,
Heaven's exalted One;
By him redemption's completed—
his chosen name is Son.

The Speaking Word

Hebrews 1:1-9

1 *Long ago, at many times and in many ways, God spoke to our fathers by the prophets,*

2 *but in these last days he has spoken to us by his Son, whom he appointed the heir of all things, through whom also he created the world.*

3 *He is the radiance of the glory of God and the exact imprint of his nature, and he upholds the universe by the word of his power. After making purification for sins, he sat down at the right hand of the Majesty on high,*

4 *having become as much superior to angels as the name he has inherited is more excellent than theirs.*

5 *For to which of the angels did God ever say,*
"You are my Son,
today I have begotten you"?
Or again,
"I will be to him a father,
and he shall be to me a son"?

6 *And again, when he brings the firstborn into the world, he says,*
"Let all God's angels worship him."

7 *Of the angels he says,*
"He makes his angels winds,
and his ministers a flame of fire."

8 *But of the Son he says,*
"Your throne, O God, is forever and ever,
the scepter of uprightness is the scepter of your kingdom.

9 *You have loved righteousness and hated wickedness;*
therefore God, your God, has anointed you with the oil of
gladness beyond your companions."

Prayer of Thanksgiving to God the Son

I praise you, O Christ, Son of the Father, for your self-sacrificing love. Leaving the glories of your eternal home. You stripped yourself of your divine privileges and spanned a chasm so vast that the angels themselves must have wondered at the sight.

To leave the bosom of the Father, with whom you had shared infinite, eternal communion, and stoop to share the agony of man's plight—lostness, darkness, wretchedness and sin—is more than words can express.

You were rich in glory; you left it all for me. You became "poor"—with a kind of poverty earth's poorest beggar knows nothing of. For you were surrounded with worship, honor, love, adoration, praise and holy dignity. You left it all. You left it voluntarily and freely. You left it joyfully behind. You were on a mission, a mission commissioned by the Father. You left the purity of light for the filth of night. You were the redeeming Agent, the Sin-bearer, the Father's sacrificial Lamb.

The long descent—not measured by time but by change, a change of clothing. The eternal Word of God putting on the clothes of the fallen creature. A servant—that is the position and posture you chose, a common servant. Sweat covered your holy brow. Dust clung to your righteous feet. A towel, a basin—you stooped to serve.

For your faithful teaching of what you had first heard from the Father; for your miracles of healing and feedings; for your wisdom, compassion, holy love, perfect example, sinless life—for all these I offer my deepest thanks.

But for the death you died for the creature's sin—even my sin—this is too much.

Amazing love! How can it be
that thou, my God, shouldst die for me?[1]

That one should die for a good man, a friend—this I can understand. But you—who are holy, harmless, undefiled and separate from sinners, and who never committed one sin—that you should die for me . . .

O for a thousand tongues to sing
My great Redeemer's praise,
The glories of my God and King,
The triumphs of His grace![2]

What can I say? What can I do? Except to say, "Thank you!" and then go out and live a life through the power of your Holy Spirit that will bring glory, honor and praise to you, the Lamb of God who has taken away the sin of the world.

Be pleased to accept this prayer of thanksgiving, O Christ. For it is only because of what you did for me on the cross, and are now doing in me by your Spirit, that I can offer this poor expression of gratitude. Amen.

Descend Upon Our Hearts

You who long ago descended
upon a seeking, waiting host,
Descend upon our hearts today—
the Father's promised Holy Ghost.

O illuminating Spirit,
O Light to darkened, blinded eyes;
Enable us to see Jesus—
Heaven's exalted, risen Prize.

O fiery Spirit of burning,
consume in us all that is dross;
Come and cleanse your prepared temples,
as we gaze upon God's own Cross.

While bending low before the Throne,
all self-rule we boldly renounce.
"Jesus is Lord," you help us pray;
this we most joyfully announce.

O Wind of God, breathe within us,
filling everyone's yielded heart;
Renew in us Christ's holy love,
leaving no inner, untouched part.

O Spirit of God, now send us
to serve others in Jesus' name;
Humbly walking before our God,
spreading abroad Christ's worthy fame.

Pleading for the Spirit

"And now, Lord, look upon their threats and grant to your servants to continue to speak your word with all boldness,
30*while you stretch out your hand to heal, and signs and wonders are performed through the name of your holy servant Jesus."*
31*And when they had prayed, the place in which they were gathered together was shaken, and they were all filled with the Holy Spirit and continued to speak the word of God with boldness.*
— Acts 4:29-31

The same disciples, who were *filled* with the Holy Spirit on the Day of Pentecost, were some of the same ones spoken of in our text, who were filled *again* with the Spirit.

Sanctification has to do with Christlike character; the filling of the Spirit has to do with power for godly living and effective service. God calls every Christian to separate himself from all ungodliness, uncleanness and sin, consecrating himself to live only and always to the glory of God. Furthermore, it is God's will to purify—and keep pure—every believer who has totally surrendered himself to the sovereign lordship of Jesus Christ. This is sanctification.

However, the level of God's manifested power, operating in the heart and life of a consecrated, sanctified Christian, ebbs and flows. The Christian is called to always walk in the Spirit, to live a Christlike life, but he will not always have the necessary power to minister effectively, unless he takes time alone, and with others, to plead for a fresh infilling of the Spirit.

Faced with severe opposition, Peter and John chose to gather with their fellow believers to plead with the sovereign Lord to pour out his Spirit afresh upon them and within them. The Lord answered the pleadings of his servants and the work of God surged forward.

How often has the work of God been defeated, in and through us, because of a failure to get alone and plead with God for a fresh infilling of the blessed Holy Spirit? These noble men and women didn't rely on a previous experience of the Spirit—as remarkable as it was—to equip them for a present crisis and challenge. They knew they needed fresh fire!

Dear friend, would you join with me—one of Christ's unworthy servants—and make the following prayer (next page) your prayer? Would you pray it until you feel it? And, then, would you pray it until you are freshly filled with the Spirit's power to do everything God has called you to do?

Prayer of Thanksgiving to God the Holy Spirit

Before I ever knew you were present, you graciously and tenderly drew me to the Father. You lovingly surrounded me like a protective cloud, forming my conscience, instructing me in the rightness and wrongness of moral choices. Although I violated your persistent voice in my tender years, still you faithfully penetrated my stubborn refusals with your gentle ways. At every turn you were there.

I thank you, Holy Spirit, for leading me to the Father through Jesus Christ, the Son. You were relentless in your pursuit. You were determined to introduce me to the Bridegroom. Your patience is unmatched. Though I tried to quiet your voice by indulging myself in lustful pursuits, you were never silent; you were always speaking.

You honored the prayers of those who interceded for me. You took their intercessions and poured out an answer by overwhelming me with a smitten, broken heart. You gave me a repentant heart. You enabled me to acknowledge my deep sinfulness. You gave me words to pray and a heart to obey. You brought me to the Father.

O gracious Spirit, I thank you for your constant companionship. You are my Helper; without you I can do nothing. You are my Strengthener; without you I am all weakness. You are my Intercessor; you take my feeble petitions to the Father, interpreting them according to your sovereign will. You are my

Teacher; without your revealed wisdom I am left in utter darkness. You are my guide through a moral morass of sin and degradation.

For every moment I have grieved you in straying from the Father's will; for every time I have chosen my own way without consulting the Father's ways; for every thought, word and deed which have fallen short of the Father's perfect standard of righteousness; for times when I have failed to act immediately when you spoke—these failures and so many more too numerable to recount—I pray for the forgiveness of the Father through Christ my Lord.

O, Holy Spirit, be pleased to continually renew my mind, producing in me the fruit of love, joy, peace, patience, kindness, goodness, faithfulness, gentleness and self-control. Whatever may hinder your ongoing, transforming ministry in me to make me more like Jesus, I pray you will send deep conviction to the depths of my heart until I shall cooperate with you implicitly in every overture you tenderly make to my soul. Make me as holy as a pardoned sinner can be.

Spirit of the living God, I bow before you in the name of Jesus, confessing my love and fidelity to you. Be pleased to accept this prayer of gratitude from one of my Lord's most unworthy servants. In the name of Christ, I pray. Amen.

Our High Priest

The ***Sympathizer*** *with our weaknesses,* (4:15; 5:2)
He was tempted in every way;
The ***Overcomer*** *of all that's evil,*
He's gentle with those gone astray.

The ***Conqueror*** *of death and destruction,* (7:24-25)
He lives as a permanent Priest;
To save sinners completely he's able,
Intercessor *for all the least.*

The ***Meeter*** *of all our deep-seated needs,* (7:26)
His credentials are unequaled;
This One who is holy, pure and blameless,
Above the heavens is exalted.

The ***Presenter*** *was he of his body,* (7:27)
Once-for-all as sin's atonement;
Of all Aaron's descendents he's ***Greater****,*
His blood was without defilement.

Royally seated at the Father's right hand, (10:12, 14)
As ***Author*** *of our salvation;*
Perfecter *of all being made holy,*
He is without comparison.

Since we have such a ***Priest*** *as Christ the Lord,* (10:19-22)
To God by him let us come near;
With faith made strong and a conscience cleansed,
Bodies washed and a heart sincere.

(Based on Letter to Hebrews.)

"Lord, make me holy . . ."

[25]Christ loved the church and gave himself up for her, [26]that he might sanctify her, having cleansed her by the washing of water with the word, [27]so that he might present the church to himself in splendor, without spot or wrinkle or any such thing, that she might be holy and without blemish.
— Ephesians 5:25-27

Christ died to save sinners; he lives to perfect saints. The first, we readily believe; the second, we are reluctant to accept.

Christ not only died for sinners, he died and lives for saints. Why did Christ die for the church?

- that he might *sanctify* the church;

- that he might *cleanse* the church by the washing of the word;

- that he might present the church to himself in splendor;

- that he might present the church to himself *without spot* or *wrinkle*;

- that the church might be *holy* and without *blemish.*

Our gracious Lord will cleanse and sanctify us to the extent we permit him. However, who among us would be bold enough to claim that he or she is absolutely without "spot or wrinkle"—without any moral defect, perfectly projecting the likeness of the Lord Jesus in every circumstance of life?

No authentic disciple of Jesus Christ makes excuses for his or herself falling short of the glory of God, regardless of one's doctrinal tradition (Wesleyan, Calvinistic, Lutheran, Catholic, Orthodox, Pentecostal, etc.).

How closely can we approximate the likeness of Christ in this world? How closely can we resemble the Lord Jesus while still clothed in these temporal fallen bodies? These are fundamental questions all sincere followers of Jesus of Nazareth grapple with. The answers to such questions do not lie in one theological system; they lie in a Person—Christ himself. Christ is our life. Christ is our hope. Christ is our wisdom, righteousness, sanctification and redemption. Christ is our advocate, friend and brother. Christ is our High Priest.

Aspiring to be all that the death, resurrection, and intercessions of Christ held for him, the prayer of 18th century Robert Murray M'Cheyne (1813-1843) cannot be improved upon: "Lord, make me as holy as a pardoned sinner can be made."[3]

Be assured: our Lord graciously responds to such cries.

Prayer for Holiness

O God, my Father, holy is your name! From all eternity the angelic hosts have cried out.

> *"Holy, holy, holy is the Lord God Almighty, who was, and is, and is to come."*

This very moment, the heavenly created beings are worshipfully singing,

> *"Holy, holy, holy."*

With the prophet of old I painfully confess,

> *"Woe is me . . . my eyes have seen the King, the LORD Almighty."*

With the trembling apostle I humbly agree,

> *"Depart from me, for I am a sinful man, O Lord."*

O righteous Father, you sent your Son to break sin's tyranny and bondage over me and in me. Christ died to set me free from Satan's cruel yoke. Jesus came to destroy the works of Satan. Sin shall not be my master, for Jesus has set me free.

By the power of your Holy Spirit penetrating my deepest need, be pleased to increasingly conform your unworthy servant to the likeness of your Son. According to your sovereign wisdom, use whatever is necessary to make me more holy: use pressure, when pressure is needed; use tests, when tests are warranted; use afflictions, when afflictions serve your higher purposes; use misunderstandings, hardships, and unfriendly providences—all to shape me and your church to more perfectly resemble the Lord Jesus.

Help me to say "yes" to you when I don't feel like surrendering. Help me to say "no" to sin when I'm inclined to enter temptation's door. By your grace abundantly working in me, help me to live constantly under your sovereign control in order that I may exercise the discipline of self-control at all times.

> *Oh, to be like Thee! Oh, to be like Thee.*
> *Blessed Redeemer, pure as Thou art!*
> *Come in Thy sweetness, come in Thy fullness;*
> *Stamp Thine own image deep on my heart.*[4]

In the strong name of Christ, your Son, I offer this prayer for myself and for your church. Amen.

The Healer

There was no hope for me—
I was unclean,
an outcast,
alone.
Then Jesus touched my flesh,
making me new without, within.

My servant could not move—
he suffered much,
paralyzed,
at home.
Then Jesus spoke a word;
I found my servant well—healed.

My wife's mother was sick—
her fever high,
she lay still,
we prayed.
Then Jesus touched her hand;
the fever fled, she rose, she served.

Demon-possessed we were—
living but dead,
tormented,
driven.
Then Jesus cried out, "Go!"
Then there came a great calm within.

I suffered for twelve years—
doctors I tried,
but grew worse,
hopeless.
Then I stooped and touched him;
Jesus said, "You're well; go in peace."

The Speaking Word

There was no hope for me . . .

And a leper came to him, imploring him, and kneeling said to him, "If you will, you can make me clean."

— Mark 1:40f

My servant could not move . . .

[5]When he entered Capernaum, a centurion came forward to him, appealing to him, [6]"Lord, my servant is lying paralyzed at home, suffering terribly."

— Matthew 8:5-6f

My wife's mother was sick . . .

[30]Now Simon's mother-in-law lay ill with a fever, and immediately they told him about her. [31]And he came and took her by the hand and lifted her up, and the fever left her, and she began to serve them.

— Mark 1:30-31

Demon-possessed we were . . .

And when he came to the other side, to the country of the Gadarenes, two demon-possessed men met him, coming out of the tombs, so fierce that no one could pass that way.

— Matthew 8:28f

I suffered for twelve years . . .

[25]And there was a woman who had had a discharge of blood for twelve years, [26]and who had suffered much under many physicians, and had spent all that she had, and was no better but rather grew worse.

— Mark 5:25-26f

Passing the Test

"Now I know that you fear God,
seeing that you have not withheld your son, your only son."
— Genesis 22:12, NIV

He was given by God
to be enjoyed
and used for his glory—
he was a gift.

And how attractive he was.
Others noticed
and applauded—
he was a gift.

I began to love him dearly.
He consumed all my moments;
I was charmed—
he was a gift.

I feared he would be taken away;
he was my treasured possession,
I clung to him tightly—
he was a gift.

Then I heard the voice.
"Surrender the gift;
return the gift."
I wept.

I traveled a long,
tortuous road.
My heart was broken.
I was about to lose my gift.

By a strength not my own,
I raised my will.
"Here is your gift;
I love you more."

He accepted back his gift,
then returned him to me.
I heard him say,
"You passed the test."

The Speaking Word

He was given by God . . .

Every good gift and every perfect gift is from above . . .

— James 1:17

And how attractive he was . . . I began to love him dearly . . .

"If anyone comes to me and does not hate his own father and mother and wife and children and brothers and sisters, yes, and even his own life, he cannot be my disciple."

— Luke 14:26

I feared he would be taken away . . .

Therefore . . . let us also lay aside every weight, and sin which clings so closely . . .

— Hebrews 12:1

Then I heard the voice . . .

"Take your son, your only son Isaac, whom you love, and go to the land of Moriah . . .

— Genesis 22:2

I traveled a long, tortuous road . . .

When they came to the place of which God had told him . . .

— Genesis 22:9

By a strength not my own . . .

"My grace is sufficient for you, for my power is made perfect in weakness."

— 2 Corinthians 12:9

He accepted back his gift . . .

[16] "By myself I have sworn, declares the LORD, because you have done this and have not withheld your son, your only son, [17] I will surely bless you . . ."

— Genesis 22:16-17

Christ Himself

More than a way out of my darkness,
more than joy in my distress;
More than a remedy for sickness—
I need Christ himself!

More than relief from a bad conscience,
more than smiling Providence;
More than a signal of his presence—
I need Christ himself!

More than mere feelings without measure,
more than blessings I treasure;
More than passing sentient pleasure—
I need Christ himself!

More than titillating sensation,
more than a revelation;
More than a brilliant visitation—
I need Christ himself!

All of these gifts absent the Giver,
leave the heart like a pauper;
Let me trust in only the Savior—
then I'll have Christ himself!

Misplaced Affection

. . . looking to Jesus, the founder and perfecter of our faith . . .
— Hebrews 12:2

There is a pitfall every disciple of the Lord Jesus Christ must constantly guard against. This pitfall is so well disguised that the new convert as well as any earnest believer may imperceptibly fall into its trap. I speak of the danger of misplaced affection: loving Christ's gifts instead of loving Christ himself.

Jesus detected this deadly flaw among many of those who presumed to follow him during his earthly ministry. After the feeding of the five thousand, Jesus and his disciples crossed the Sea of Galilee. The following day, many of the beneficiaries of that miracle traveled miles in search of Jesus. When they found Jesus, he intuitively knew why they had come. They were in search of Christ's gifts instead of seeking Christ for who he was; they only came to Jesus for what he could do for them: "Truly, truly I say to you, you are seeking me, not because you saw signs, but because you ate your fill of the loaves" (John 6:26).

The same ulterior motive pervades the church's landscape today. Many uninstructed, immature believers are lusting after the next miracle, blessing, dynamic worship service. These zealous souls are so preoccupied with what they want Christ to *do* for them that they give little or any thought about getting to *know* Christ through the Gospel accounts and the fellowship of the Holy Spirit.

The language of the apostle is foreign to these uninformed souls: "Indeed, I count everything as loss because of the surpassing worth of knowing Christ Jesus my Lord" (Phil. 3:8). For Paul, the Lord Jesus was always at the *center.*

The living Christ never comes to an honest, seeking heart without also bringing with him those moral attributes and spiritual gifts he chooses to sovereignly distribute. However, let the growing, maturing disciple learn to never misplace his affections. While he is grateful to his merciful Lord for every good and perfect gift that comes down from above, let him love the *Giver* more than the gifts, the *Blesser* more than the blessing, the *Maker* more than the miracle, the *Deliverer* more than the deliverance, the *Healer* more than the healing.

In the words of the New Testament writer, let us always be "looking to Jesus" (Heb. 12:2).

Oh, That I May Know You

Oh, that I may know you, O Christ,
in your resurrection power—
The pow'r that brought you from the grave,
triumphant in your darkest hour.

Without you, all-conquering One,
I'm fruitless, alone, dry and bare.
Except I know your inner strength,
my love is cold, my service rare.

Contemplating your holiness,
I know I'm utterly defiled.
But you nailed my sin to your cross;
now with my God I'm reconciled.

With you, O Christ, I am buried;
with you, I rose from the dark tomb.
Because you overcame that Day,
my life is no more shrouded with gloom.

Oh, that I may know you, O Christ,
in your resurrection power—
Know you more and more ev'ry day,
walking with you hour by hour.

Oh, that I may know you, O Christ,
in your resurrection power—
Until the day you take me Home,
when I'll know you so much clearer.

Knowing Christ

I want to know Christ . . .
— Philippians 3:10, NIV

A person who views God as only a curious object to be studied instead of the infinite Father who desires fellowship with each member of the human family, thinks it foolhardy when hearing Christ's disciples speak of *knowing* Christ. After all, wasn't Jesus of Nazareth killed and buried two thousand years ago? How can one *know* a dead man whom they've never met?

Saul of Tarsus must have thought the same thing before his Christ-encounter on the Damascus Road. However, that one personal revelation of the resurrected, living Christ immediately transformed the mistaken theology of this radical rabbi, thrusting him into a lifelong quest. He had seen Christ with his own eyes; he heard Christ with his own ears. Now he must seek to *know* this one who knows this chief of sinners so well.

Even the greatest of the church's saints have never been able to fully *comprehend* God (the finite is incapable of fully comprehending the Infinite). But God can be *known*; not perfectly, but intimately and increasingly by those who maintain a healthy spiritual appetite for him. And we grow in our knowledge of God as we walk in the light of God: "in your light do we see light" (Psalm 36:9).

Thirty years after Paul's meeting the Lord Jesus, he is sitting in a Roman prison dictating a letter to the Philippian Christians. By now a seasoned veteran of the Cross, his love for Christ is undiminished. Yet he longs to know Christ in a deeper reality. Paul writes, "I want to know Christ . . ." (Phil. 3:10, NIV). Think of it, here's the church's foremost apostle, apologist, and evangelist confessing to his one paramount driving desire: "I want to know Christ." A. W Tozer (1897-1963) called this the "soul's paradox of love." He wrote: "To have found God and still pursue Him is the soul's paradox of love, scorned indeed by the too-easily-satisfied religionist, but justified in happy experience by the children of the burning heart."[5]

The same word Paul used for "know" in Philippians 3:10 is a cognate form of the same Greek word rendered "knew" in the *Septuagint* (Greek version of the Hebrew Old Testament) in Genesis 4:1: "Now Adam knew his wife Eve . . ." The physical intimacy expressed between a husband and wife is analogous to the spiritual knowledge and intimacy every thirsty-hearted disciple longs for in his or her relation to the living Christ.

When this desire to know Christ more fully wanes and recedes in the heart of the true believer, proactive steps must be taken to rekindle this fiery passion lest this love for our Lord grow cold.

Let my passion always be . . . to *know* Christ.

My Advocate and Friend

"Even now my witness is in heaven;
my advocate is on high; my intercessor is my friend
as my eyes pour out tears to God . . ."
— Job 16:19-20, NIV

[1]My little children, I am writing these things to you so that you may not sin. And if anyone sins, we have an Advocate with the Father, Jesus Christ the righteous; [2]and He Himself is the propitiation for our sins and not for ours only, but also for those of the whole world.
— I John 2:1-2, NASB

I have no plea, for God's righteous Law I've broken—
the holy word is plain to see;
his will was fully known by me.
What can I do, where can I flee?

The Law shouts, "You must die; no pardon can there be!
God's word is absolute for all;
there is no exception, no recall.
The verdict is plain: you must go!"

Then I heard a surer sound, one above the rest:
"I sent my Son to take your place;
I filled him full of truth and grace.
Christ speaks for you; his blood avails."

The ever-living One dwells at the Father's side.
He shows his wounds when I have failed,
to plead my cause when I'm assailed.
Christ is my Friend! His blood avails!

The Christian's Advocates

According to the Word of God coming through the apostle John—one of Christ's most intimate, earthly companions—the Christian has two Advocates. The one is the Lord Jesus Christ, who is presently seated at the right hand of God the Father, "we have an Advocate with the Father, Jesus Christ the righteous . . ." (1 John 2:1); the other is the Holy Spirit, who indwells every true believer, "And I will ask the Father, and he will give you another Advocate. . . . You know him, for he dwells with you and will be in you" (John 14:17, RIT).

The Greek word in these two texts translated above as "Advocate," is variously rendered by Bible translators: Advocate, Helper, Comforter, Counselor. The word means "one who comes to a person's aid; one who speaks in someone's defense."

The believer's Advocate seated at the Father's right hand is none other than the crucified, risen, ascended Christ of God. He serves as the Christian's mediator and intercessor. What he meritoriously effected on the Cross, he preserves and maintains through his mediatorial office as our Great High Priest. In the words of Charles Wesley (1707-1788):

He ever lives above,
For me to intercede;
His all redeeming love,
His precious blood to plead.

Again,

Five bleeding wounds he bears,
Received on Calvary;
They pour effectual prayers,
They strongly plead for me.[6]

Centuries before the Word was made flesh, died, arose, and ascended to the Father's side to serve as the believer's Advocate, the suffering Job was given a glimpse of such an intercessor:

"Even now my witness is in heaven; my advocate is on high; my intercessor is my friend as my eyes pour out tears to God ..." (Job 16:19-20, NIV). Unlike many of Christ's distressed followers today, this Old Testament blameless believer had the overwhelming confidence that his Advocate was also his friend.

As Christians, when is it we are in need of our heavenly Advocate? "But if anyone does sin . . ." (1 John 2:1). Some of us go to great exegetical lengths to define the "if" in this text. Others endlessly try to explain what John means precisely by "sin." Then there are the children-at-heart—these simply look up to their *Friend* and *Advocate* on high whenever the indwelling *Advocate* gives them a gentle nudge. These are the truly forgiven. These live in peace. These are the confident children of God.

My Brothers

These are my brothers:
being made more and more like me;
Renewed in my very image,
is their destiny.

These are my brothers:
ashamed of them I will not be;
They are children of my Father—
all one family.

These are my brothers:
in their midst I declare your name;
Among them I sing your praises,
exulting in your fame.

These are my brothers:
who went through life afraid to die;
For these the bondage I've broken,
destroying the Lie.

These are my brothers:
of their humanity I share;
That I merciful and faithful,
show to them I care.

These are my brothers:
to help I am always able;
Because I was tempted as well,
they need not stumble.

Unashamed

For he who sanctifies and those who are sanctified all have one origin. That is why he is not ashamed to call them brothers . . .
— Hebrews 2:11

I experienced an unexpected epiphany (aren't all epiphanies unexpected?) recently while sitting in a local restaurant watching my four-year-old grandson entertaining himself in the adjoining play area.

Luke had quickly made friends with another boy while the two frolicked on the assortment of play equipment designed for small children. After the boys had made their way a number of times up the steps and down the slide, they ran over to the glass panel which separated the booth where I was sitting from the play area. Pointing to me while wearing a big smile, Luke said to his new friend, "That's my PawPaw!" I returned the smile, then the two were off to play again.

Being the young child that he is, Luke undoubtedly never gave that spontaneous, affectionate interlude another thought. Not so with me. Days later I'm still basking in its glow, having already shared the event with several willing—or, unwilling—listeners.

But I was left to wonder. With my mind filled with cascading thoughts—thoughts of love and affection I felt for this boy, and the affection he had instinctively and publicly expressed for his grandfather in the presence of a stranger—my mind went back to one of the most remarkable statements spoken about the Lord Jesus in all of God's Word: "he is not ashamed to call them brothers . . ." (Heb. 2:11).

Quoting selections from Psalms and Isaiah, the Spirit-inspired writer of the Epistle of Hebrews says the Lord Jesus exults in his solidarity with his "brothers" (the ancient Greek term often included both genders and is used three times in this passage: verses 11, 12, 17). The God-made-flesh—who suffered and was tempted and died, who "was made like his brothers in every respect, so that he might be a merciful and faithful high priest . . ."—is not ashamed to identify with his Father's children, because all those "he . . . sanctifies and those who are sanctified . . . have their origin in one Father."

If a little boy, without inhibition, hesitation or embarrassment, proudly announced his relationship to a man almost six decades older than he sitting in a restaurant, how much more will the Lord Jesus ultimately, finally and joyfully announce his relationship to his Father's children before a watching universe.

The church too often has been an embarrassment to its Head. By his moment-by-moment imparted grace, let us who are called by his name purpose daily to live in this present evil world so our Elder Brother is not ashamed to recognize us as one of his own.

Christ is Victor!

The secret of our inner strength
within us does not lie;
The power to say no to sin
must descend from on high.

Our wills are diseased, very frail,
intentions but futile—
Unless we let the Lord prevail,
reigning without rival.

Self-willed efforts are all vain,
resolves but a vapor.
Blood and fire are what are needed—
forgiveness and power.

The blood was shed by Christ himself,
cleansing all the conscience.
The fire blazed strong at Pentecost,
infusing holy pow'r.

Christ, and Christ alone is Victor,
he triumphed o'er his foes;
He defeated all man's rivals
at the Cross, then arose.

Let us turn from self-dependence,
before the Cross lying;
Let us surrender control to
Jesus, on him relying.

Flesh or Spirit?

But I say, walk by the Spirit, and you will not gratify the desires of the flesh.
— Galatians 5:16

When the apostle Paul uses the term "flesh," he uses it as a metaphor to describe man's thinking and acting as a *mere* man, a mere person. The "flesh" consists of attitudes, thoughts, and behavior contrary to the Spirit. But the "flesh" is more than attitudes, thoughts, and behavior, it is what we *are* apart from the active presence of the Spirit of God in our lives.

In describing the human condition prior to the Flood, the Lord announced his verdict for that age, "My Spirit shall not strive with man forever, because *in his going astray he is flesh"* (Gen 6:3; literal translation in italics). Commentators Keil-Delitzsch remark: "Men, says God, have proved themselves by their erring and straying to be flesh, i.e., given up to flesh, and incapable of being ruled by the Spirit of God and led back to the divine goal of their life."[7] That pre-flood generation was so dominated by its animal appetites that God called man as a genus "flesh."

The apostle Paul, under the inspiration of the Spirit, submits a partial list of the "works of the flesh"—those attitudes and behaviors that characterize a variety of people who are not living life in harmony with the Spirit: "Now the works of the flesh are evident: sexual immorality, impurity, sensuality, idolatry, sorcery, enmity, strife, jealousy, fits of anger, rivalries, dissensions, divisions, envy, drunkenness, orgies, and things like these . . ." (Gal. 5:19-20).

The above manifestations of the "flesh" (in Noah's age and Paul's list) are what we normally think of when we think of people who act and live according to basic human instincts and do not serve under the Spirit's control. But, for *religious* people, there are more subtle, but nonetheless real, attitudes and actions of the "flesh" that too often influence our thinking and control our behavior.

Before the Spirit invaded his own life, the apostle Paul's ultimate and real confidence was in the "flesh"—religious activities—and not in God. The fact was, Paul said if he chose to, he could boast about his religious pedigree: "circumcised on the eighth day, of the people of Israel, of the tribe of Benjamin, a Hebrew of Hebrews; as to the law, a Pharisee; as to zeal, a persecutor of the church; as to righteousness, under the law blameless . . ." (Phil. 3:5-6).

We have a choice to either glorify Christ or ourselves. We will either be people of the "flesh" or Spirit-people. God save us and our churches from the former, and may the latter multiply abundantly among us.

My Shepherd's Voice

Above and beyond the din of this world,
a Voice is heard; I hear its sound.
Turning my soul from all other noises,
I'm anxious to hear what he discloses—
it is my Shepherd's voice.

I have no fear; he never comes to scold.
For his heart is full of mercy
And his wisdom is suited perfectly.
I've learned to trust him implicitly—
it is my Shepherd's voice.

Faithfully he warns of predators,
which are stalking my every move.
"Abide in Me," he says so distinctly.
With word and faith he arms me securely—
it is my Shepherd's voice.

Empty of inner strength, I hear him speak,
bidding me to a quiet place.
Turning aside I find a meal prepared;
I eat and drink and am refreshed—
it is my Shepherd's voice.

Whenever I've strayed—ever so slightly—
I hear his tones, both true and clear.
He bids me return to the narrow path,
to follow him with unwavering faith—
it is my Shepherd's voice.

On those days when all feels dark and dreadful,
a reassuring echo comes.
Pointing me to unfailing promises,
he fills me with rapturous choruses—
it is my Shepherd's voice.

On that Day—not too far in the distance—
before the Judge of all I'll stand.
To hear him pronounce, "Well done, my servant,"
will be a sound of all sounds most pleasant—
it is my Shepherd's voice.

Prayer and Listening

And Samuel said, "Speak, for your servant hears."
— 1 Samuel 3:10

Much that is said and written about prayer fails to note the importance of listening—listening to the voice of the Good Shepherd during the quiet time.

Prayer is many things. Prayer includes the praise and worship of God; it involves thanksgiving and expressions of gratitude for every good and perfect gift coming down from above. Prayer often takes the form of supplication and intercession; it knows what it is to intercede before God with upraised hands while the Joshuas are on the fields of battle, warring against the enemy. There are also times when prayer consists in no more than groans being poured out before a merciful God, groans incapable of articulating one's petitions before an omniscient God.

Prayer is also listening—listening to hear the voice of the Spirit coming through the Word of God written, listening to hear the voice of the Spirit speaking in order to apply the Word of God to one's particular circumstances.

Daily listening prayer takes time—unhurried, uncluttered, all alone, quietness—time. Time spent in solitude with God, with his Word. Bible reading should be a devotional exercise which is done while praying all the while one is reading, meditating, and contemplating. The maturing disciple of the Lord Jesus is learning to listen to the voice of the Shepherd as he reads Spirit-inspired truth.

It is possible to read the written Word of God without ever hearing the voice of God, just as people often heard the voice of the Word-made-flesh two millennia ago with their outer ears, but never actually embraced his spoken truth with their inner ears. Thus we hear the Lord Jesus often ending his messages during his earthly ministry with the exhortation: "He who has an ear to hear, let him hear."

One of the undeniable axioms of the kingdom of God is this: Christ's most intimate friends are those who have learned to be good listeners: "My sheep hear my voice, and I know them, and they follow me" (John 10:27).

If you do not already practice *listening prayer* as you read God's sacred Word, try doing so the next time. Moreover, when leaving the place of daily solitude, learn to cultivate the spiritual exercise of listening to the *Voice* throughout the day.

Too much of what we have called prayer is only one-way communication, which in reality is no communication. We have done most of the talking. Let us now begin to listen—listen to the voice of the Spirit speaking through his Word, and then obediently applying his words of wisdom in life's routines and crises.

I Long to Know You, O Christ!

More than a historical figure,
More than a word on paper,
More than a tradition to savor—
I long to know you, O Christ!

More than a text for my mind to cite,
More than a creed that is right,
More than a prayer to recite—
I long to know you, O Christ!

More than a distant tale to be told,
More than one event grown cold,
More than desiring celestial gold—
I long to know you, O Christ!

More than a church to which I belong,
More than a mission I'm on,
More than a cause righting the wrong—
I long to know you, O Christ!

More than a mere doctrine to be taught,
More than a gift to be sought,
More than an experience inwrought—
I long to know you, O Christ!

More than clear principles to pursue,
More than self to keep in view,
More than an upright life that is true—
I long to know you, O Christ!

Knowing Christ Personally

Indeed, I count everything as loss because of the surpassing worth of knowing Christ Jesus my Lord.
— Philippians 3:8

Noted evangelical theologian, J.I. Packer, wrote: "I walked in the sunshine with a scholar who had effectively forfeited his prospects of academic advancement by clashing with church dignitaries over the gospel of grace. 'But it doesn't matter,' he said at length, 'for I've known God and they haven't.' "[8] Packer said the man's remark caused him to do a great deal of thinking. Such thinking resulted in his writing *Knowing God*, a book now considered a classic in its field.

No one, including the greatest of the church's saints, has ever been able to fully *comprehend* God (the finite is incapable of fully comprehending the Infinite). But the Bible affirms that God can be *known*—not perfectly, not absolutely, but he can be known by those to whom he reveals himself—to those who cultivate a healthy spiritual appetite for him. "Because God is infinite and we are finite or limited," writes systematic theologian Wayne Grudem, "we can never fully understand God." Grudem further explains: "In this sense God is said to be *incomprehensible*, where the term *incomprehensible* is used with an older and less common sense, 'unable to be fully understood.'" Grudem then adds: "This sense must be clearly distinguished from the more common meaning, 'unable to be understood.' It is not true to say that God is unable to be understood, but it is true to say that he cannot be understood fully or exhaustively."[9]

So while God cannot be known exhaustively, in the sense of fully understanding him, nonetheless, he can be known—known *personally*. God has chosen through the centuries to grant a limited knowledge to man by revealing himself in a number of ways—through natural creation, the Law and the prophets, signs and miracles, and the conscience. However, God's ultimate revelation of himself culminated in the Incarnation—"the Word became flesh and dwelt among us . . ." (John 1:14).

In the coming of the Lord Jesus Christ, God's Son walked among men and women to more perfectly reveal what God was like: "No one has ever seen God; the only God, who is at the Father's side has made him known" (John 1:18). Thus, to see Christ was to see God—in a limited measure—but the most "limited measure" man had ever experienced until that point in history. As the apostle would later write, "For in him all the fullness of God was pleased to dwell" (Col. 1:19). And as Jesus himself once explained to an inquiring disciple who asked to see the Father: "Have I been with you so long, and you still do not know me, Philip? Whoever has seen me has seen the Father" (Jo. 14:9).

Do you *know* Christ personally, dear reader? Are you seeking to know him more intimately?

Oh, the Very Love of Christ

Oh, the very love of Christ
in my heart is shed abroad;
Filling each void and closet,
making music to my God.

Oh, Christ's all-consuming love
renews me in God's image;
Sanctifying all it fills
as I gaze on his visage.

Oh, amazing love of Christ,
I would know in its fullness—
Its depth and breadth, length and height,
its mercy and forgiveness.

Oh, the selfless love of Christ
penetrates springs of action;
Shaping the innermost self
until there's Christlike motion.

Oh, to know more of Christ's love,
my heart yearns with great passion;
May this be my constant prayer,
controlling my volition.

The Love of Christ

May you experience the love of Christ,
though it is too great to understand fully.
— Ephesians 3:19, NLT

Of all the prayer requests I've heard in more than 38 years of pastoral ministry, I have heard few requests quite like the apostle Paul's (see above). I have listened to a litany of health-related requests. I have heard requests for physical protection and job promotions; for passing grades and material success, but a prayer request for someone to experience the love of Christ is rare.

Why is this so? Because we're so material-conscious. The average 21st century Christian living in the Western world, is so preoccupied with earning a living, making investments, saving for retirement, acquiring the latest gadgets—that if and when he does show up for a prayer meeting, he instinctively thinks in material terms when requests are solicited, because he's consumed by the material.

We cannot experience the love of Christ if our heart is filled with the love of the world and the things in the world. It is one thing for us to possess things; it is another for things to possess us. Christ earnestly desires to possess us. Christ wants to fill our hearts with his very own love.

My greatest ongoing need is to experience the love of

Christ—the pure, selfless love of Christ. For in experiencing the love of Christ, I am enabled to think of others more highly than I think of myself; I am empowered to bear with my brother and sister's short-comings and failures. By being filled with Christ's love, life's petty annoyances and irritations are almost nil. What would normally frustrate and exasperate me, is borne with ease when enjoying the love of Christ.

How often I have fallen short because I failed to wait in God's presence until my heart was replenished with Christ's love. How many careless words have been spoken, how many ill-conceived decisions have been made—simply because we acted before we gazed upon the face of Christ.

Prayer: *Too often, O Christ, I have tried to do your work without experiencing your all-consuming love. Forgive me. Grant to your servant such an appetite for you, that nothing less than you will ever satisfy—nothing less than your very own love. Amen.*

At the Foot of the Cross

As a new day dawns I take my chosen place
At the foot of the Cross where Christ died for me.
With a penitent heart, pressing low my face,
My arms embrace his death that sets sinners free.
Gazing upon Christ's loveliness,
Confessing my unworthiness,
Beseeching his forgiveness—
My soul becomes lost in love and accolades.

While I linger here in holy solitude
Meditating upon my Father's mercies,
My soul is transported to the heavenlies
As God fills it with delightful ecstasies.
Applauding his Son's position,
Thanking him for his creation,
Exalting him for salvation—
I could lie here worshiping all my days.

It's at the foot of the Cross I'm reminded
Of my Father's costly investment in me:
The sacrificial death of his unique Son,
Their breach in communion momentarily.
Speechlessly, my heart is amazed,
Breathlessly, my spirit is raised,
Adoringly, my mind is dazed—
As I wonder at the Lord God and his ways.

Reluctantly, I rise from our trysting site,
Made holy by his sanctifying presence.
But he draws me to return to this world
To serve his church and others with his fragrance.
Renewed by his Spirit freshly,
Filled with the love of Christ warmly,
Called to exalt my Lord only—
I take my cross gladly to live to his praise.

The Daily Tryst

Behold what manner of love the Father has bestowed on us, that we should be called children of God!
— 1 John 3:1, NKJV

Just as there is a reciprocation of romantic love between two lovers, so there is an exchange of *agape* love between the heavenly Father and all of his children who have been born of his Spirit. However, the Father's love toward his offspring is so much greater and consistent than is his children's love toward him. Nevertheless, however defective and intermittent the love of the child may be, it is still love and it is still accepted by the Father.

When the repentant Christian comes alive to God in regenerating grace, the love of God is poured into the new believer's heart (see Romans 5:5). Consequently, such a one can testify with the beloved apostle, "We love Him because He first loved us" (1 John 4:19, NKJV).

For those lovers who love one another on the human and natural level, it is important if their love is to deepen and grow for one another that they meet often, that they take time with one another. Such couples demand regular appointed places of meeting—*trysts,* if you will.

The term *tryst* is a noun and a verb. When used as a noun, it means an agreement (as between lovers) to meet; when used as a verb, it means to make or keep a tryst. The word derives its origin from Scandinavia and originally meant *trust.*

The new believer soon learns the value of keeping a daily tryst with his divine Lover. He or she would as soon go without food and drink as to miss spending time alone with the Father. This tryst does not spring from law and duty, it is born and maintained by love—*agape* love—the very same love that led Christ to get alone with his Father on the mountain.

Continuous communion is to be the goal and experience for every growing Christian, but continuous communion must be maintained and renewed through the daily tryst. It is there the Lover speaks to the loved one through his Word, and the loved one speaks to the Lover through prayer.

Lovers love spending time together. Even when they part, they're really together—in each other's thoughts. But it's as though they can't wait for the next tryst.

Do we love the Father? Do we carefully guard our daily tryst with him? Can God trust you to keep your *trysts*?

All We Need

God's mercies are new morning by morning;
without end his faithfulness he displays.
From his right side rich blessings are flowing
to all who live only to his Son's praise.

Grace in abundance, peace beyond measure—
roll like torrents from his throne through the Cross,
So that not one in whom he takes pleasure
should ever have reason to suffer loss.

Infinite love that defies description
is lavished on those who cherish his Son;
Kindness which shuns every limitation,
he freely gives out to all he has won.

With such vast wealth surrounding his children,
why should our days be so heavy with care?
Do we not know our Father in Heaven
has all we need and is willing to share?

So let us go daily, time and again,
asking simply for what we stand in need;
Knowing our requests will not be in vain,
because he loves both in word and in deed.

The Speaking Word

God's mercies are new morning by morning . . .

[22]Through the LORD's mercies we are not consumed, Because His compassions fail not. [23]They are new every morning; great is Your faithfulness.

— Lamentations 3:22-23, NKJV

Grace in abundance, peace beyond measure . . .

May grace and peace be multiplied to you.

— 1 Peter 1:2

Infinite love that defies description . . .

Behold what manner of love the Father has bestowed on us, that we should be called children of God!

— 1 John 3:1, NKJV

With such vast wealth surrounding his children . . .

But seek first the kingdom of God and his righteousness, and all these things will be added to you.

— Matthew 6 33

So let us go daily, time and again . . .

"Ask, and it will be given to you . . ."

— Matthew 7:7

Jesus is Risen

Jesus is risen;
the veil's been torn.
New life he's given;
praise to the Lord!
Christ interceding;
for me is pleading.
He's all I'm needing—
the living Word.

Morning has broken;
the Word has spoken.
Manna from Heaven,
feeding my soul.
Cleansing my nature,
strength for my labor,
Guiding my future—
he's in control.

Gazing on Jesus,
seeing my weakness;
Changed to his likeness,
daily I plead.
Walking in union,
blessed communion,
Serving his mission
to those in need.

Soon I'll be leaving,
this world receding;
Jesus awaiting,
oh, what a Lamb!
Amazing story,
Christ in his glory!
His wounds before me,
unworthy I am.

(Sung to the tune "Morning Has Broken.")

The Speaking Word

Jesus is risen . . .

"Men of Israel, hear these words: Jesus of Nazareth, a man attested to you by God with mighty works and wonders and signs that God did through him in your midst, as you yourselves know— [23]this Jesus, delivered up according to the definite plan and foreknowledge of God, you crucified and killed by the hands of lawless men. [24]God raised him up, loosing the pangs of death, because it was not possible for him to be held by it."

— Acts 2:22-24

Morning has broken . . .

O LORD, in the morning you hear my voice; in the morning I prepare a sacrifice for you and watch.

— Psalm 5:3

Gazing on Jesus . . .

[1]Therefore, since we have so great a cloud of witnesses surrounding us, let us also lay aside every encumbrance and the sin which so easily entangles us, and let us run with endurance the race that is set before us, [2]fixing our eyes on Jesus, the author and perfecter of faith, who for the joy set before him endured the cross, despising the shame, and has sat down at the right hand of the throne of God.

— Hebrews 12:1-2

Soon I'll be leaving . . .

Behold, you have made my days a few handbreadths, and my lifetime is as nothing before you. Surely all mankind stands as a mere breath!

— Psalm 39:5

My Deepest Need

What is my deepest need
when I kneel to pray—
Is it for temporal goods,
for vessel made of clay?

It's true, the Master taught
I am to ask for bread,
And should illness be my lot—
have elders anoint my head.

Nothing is ever too small
to escape my Father's care.
Reluctant I should not be—
all to take to him in prayer.

But what is my deepest need
when I kneel to pray—
Is it for temporal goods,
for vessel made of clay?

Is not my deepest need,
when bowing low in prayer,
To confess my need for mercy,
since debts are always there?

Should any child of God presume—
"Perfection is now complete;
I always hit the mark of love;
asking for mercy is obsolete"?

No, my Father in Heaven explains,
when coming before his throne,
My deepest need is mercy—
without which I stand alone.

The Mercy of God

Let us then with confidence draw near to the throne of grace, that we may receive mercy and find grace to help in time of need.
— Hebrews 4:16

Without a merciful God there is neither pardon for the sinner nor hope for the believer. Of the sinner, Paul writes, "But when the goodness and loving kindness of God our Savior appeared, he saved us, not because of works done by us in righteousness, but according to his own mercy . . ." (Titus 3:4-5); of the believer, Hebrews says, "Let us then with confidence draw near to the throne of grace, that we may receive mercy and find grace to help in time of need" (4:16). The Titus passage refers to repentant sinners, the Hebrews text, to believers.

While all Christians, regardless of their ecclesiastical roots, would have admitted to their need of God's mercy when they initially repented of their sins and received God's gracious forgiveness, not all Christians are persuaded they are continually in need of God's mercy, for not all Christians are convinced they fall short of God's glory (see Rom. 3:23). So, if one does not believe he falls short of God's glory, it is only logical that he does not feel the need of God's moment-by-moment mercy. This is the curse of the aberrational teaching of *sinless* perfectionism—something John Wesley (1703-1791) never taught, though many of his followers do.

While sailing across the Atlantic to America with Mr. Oglethorpe, who was to be the governor of the new colony of Georgia, John Wesley heard a noise in the governor's cabin. So Wesley went to the cabin, and the governor said, "I dare say you want to know what this noise is about, sir; I have good occasion for it. You know, sir, that the only wine I drink is Cyprus wine, and it is necessary for me; I put it on board, and this rascal, my servant, this Grimaldi, has drunken all of it; I will have him beaten on the deck, and the first ship of war that comes by, he shall be taken by press, and enlisted in His Majesty's service, and a hard time he shall have of it, for I will let him know that I never forgive." "Your honor," said Mr. Wesley, "then I hope you never sin."

The rebuke was so well put, so pointed, and so needed, that the governor replied in a moment, "Alas, sir, I do sin, and I have sinned in what I have said; for your sake he shall be forgiven; I trust he will not do the like again."[10]

Our Lord taught his disciples to pray, "Forgive us our debts" (Mt. 6:12). Since as Christians we are obligated to always *pay* God and others only love (see Rom. 13:10), therefore, when we fail to love God and others perfectly, we incur a debt.

Only the self-righteous never incur debts and therefore have none to confess.

God of Mercy

God of mercy,
God of might,
fill your child
with your pure light.

God all-holy,
God of grace,
cleanse my heart;
show me your face.

God of living,
God of life,
breathe in me;
remove all strife.

God of wisdom,
God of fire,
purge my will
and my desire.

God all-perfect,
God all-right,
sanctify
me in your sight.

God all-loving,
God most kind,
conform me
to Christ's own mind.

God of wonder,
God of days,
fill my mouth
with endless praise.

God exalted,
God most high,
be my guest,
forever nigh.

God almighty,
God all-strong,
keep me free
from ev'ry wrong.

God all-able,
God my rock,
preserve me
with all your flock.

Thoughts on God

"Whoever has seen me has seen the Father . . ."
— John 14:9

One of the first books I purchased after coming to Christ was A. W. Tozer's (1897-1963) *The Knowledge of the Holy*. Doubtless this little volume—which is now considered a classic—is one of the best on the subject of the attributes of God. In introducing his readers to this worthy subject matter, Tozer said, "Without doubt, the mightiest thought the mind can entertain is the thought of God, and the weightiest word in any language is its word for God."[11]

The God, of course, Tozer was speaking of is the God who is the Creator of all things; the God of Abraham, Isaac, and Jacob; the God and Father of the Lord Jesus Christ; the God in trinity: Father, Son, and Holy Spirit; the God who revealed himself decisively through the incarnation of his Son; the God who inspired holy men to write the sacred Scriptures.

The Bible speaks of God's self-existence, self-sufficiency, eternity, infinitude, immutability, immensity, omniscience, omnipotence, omnipresence, wisdom, transcendence, immanence, faithfulness, goodness, righteousness and justice, mercy, grace, holiness, love, sovereignty, and so much more.

When thinking on this subject of God, somewhere from the well of my mind there surfaced Adam Clarke's (1762-1842) attempt at defining God. Methodism's first commentator on the Holy Scriptures acknowledged that a perfect definition was impossible, but he made the venture just the same (on Genesis 1:1).

> The eternal, independent, and self-existent Being: the Being whose purposes and actions spring from himself, without foreign motive or influence: he who is absolute in dominion; the most pure, the most simple, and most spiritual of all essences; infinitely benevolent, beneficent, true, and holy: the cause of all being, the upholder of all things; infinitely happy, because infinitely perfect; and eternally self-sufficient, needing nothing that he has made: illimitable in his immensity, inconceivable in his mode of existence, and indescribable in his essence; known fully only to himself, because an infinite mind can be fully apprehended only by itself. In a word, a Being who, from his infinite wisdom, cannot err or be deceived; and who, from his infinite goodness, can do nothing but what is eternally just, right, and kind.[12]

While the Bible nowhere gives us a definition of God, the Bible does provide us with a multi-faceted account of who God is and what God is like. We see definitively what God is like when look upon the Christ of God, as recorded in the Gospels and revealed by the Spirit: "Whoever has seen me has seen the Father" (John 14:9).

Prayer: *Lord, open my eyes.*

Surprised by Mercy

He left home and wandered far,
then decided to return,
wondering if his father
would hold it against him.
He was surprised by Mercy.

He was pronounced "unclean"
because of a dreadful disease;
shamed, isolated, ridiculed,
his life was full of misery.
He was surprised by Mercy.

He was a captive of Satan,
tormented day and night;
chained, raging, and possessed,
a prisoner of evil choices.
He was surprised by Mercy.

She was a disreputable person,
condemned by all who knew her,
having lived with many men;
that day at the well her life was changed.
She was surprised by Mercy.

He was part of the inner circle,
but in a crisis of choice
he sorely failed, turning away;
heartbroken, he looked back and saw those eyes.
He was surprised by Mercy.

His life was about to end,
capital death was his due;
there was no time to change,
then he heard, "Today . . ."
He was surprised by Mercy.

He was only a young man,
sixteen at the time—
lost, confused, and seeking—
then Jesus passed by.
I *was surprised by Mercy.*

The Father of Mercies

"And his mercy is for those who fear him from generation to generation."
— Luke 1:50

While recently meditating on the narratives in Luke 1, I was struck by the recurrence of the word "mercy." I shouldn't have been, I suppose, for after all, this passage recounts two resplendent, grace-filled events immediately preceding the miraculous birth of our Lord.

The first brief story informs us of an elderly Jewish couple who had no children. We are told that the husband, Zechariah, served his Lord as a priest in the temple, and that his wife, Elizabeth, was a descendant of Aaron, Israel's first high priest.

While Zechariah was ministering in the temple one notable day, he received a startling visit by an angel, informing him that not only would he and Elizabeth become parents in their old age, but that their son would play a special role in preparing God's people for the promised Messiah. Though he initially responded in disbelief to the angel's announcement, nine months later this righteous priest sang a Spirit-induced hymn, punctuated with the theme of *mercy*:

> *"Blessed be the Lord God of Israel, for he has visited and redeemed his people . . . to show the **mercy** promised to our fathers . . ."* (1:68, 72).

Then, looking into the face of his newborn son, he sings:

"And you, child, will be called the prophet of the Most High; for you will go before the Lord to prepare his ways, to give knowledge of salvation to his people in the forgiveness of their sins, because of the tender ***mercy*** *of our God . . ."* (1:76-78).

The next story involves the mother of our Lord, Mary. Following Gabriel's incomparable announcement to the young virgin that she was to be the human bearer of the Christ child, she rushed to tell Elizabeth the Good News. After greetings were exchanged, Mary burst forth in song, exulting in the mercy of God:

"And his ***mercy*** *is for those who fear him from generation to generation "* (1:50).

"He has helped his servant Israel, in remembrance of his ***mercy*** *. . ."* (1:54).

Is it any wonder, then, that the early church's foremost persecutor, who was later surprised by God's mercy, calls this very same God, "the Father of mercies" (2 Cor. 1:3)?

Grace

Grace: The Father's generous favor toward those
deserving nothing but death and hell.
In the loving heart of God was it conceived—
is freely given to all who fell.

Grace: The Son's very life was uniquely given
for all sheep who have wandered away;
Through Christ's blood it is offered
to all who renounce sin, self and pray.

Grace: The Spirit's sole mandate and faithful mission
is to communicate the Father's plan,
Drawing sinners to the Lord—
conforming each to the perfect Man.

Grace: God's mighty power operating within,
strengthening us the Lamb to honor,
Alone . . . we are defeated,
filled with grace we go forth to conquer.

Grace: Which key is it unlocking this special door?
How can redeemed sinners receive more?
Then I heard the Master say,
"Become as a child—humility."

Always Grace!

For we are the aroma of Christ to God among those who are being saved . . .
— 2 Corinthians 2:15

From beginning to end the Christian life is a product of divine grace. We are debtors, and will always be, to our Creator-Redeemer, who formed us in our mother's womb, birthed in us our first thoughts of him, drew us to Calvary's cross, enabled us to trust in his Son, and sustains and preserves us as we run this race of all races.

God is debtor to no man, but the saved will be forever indebted to God. For the one who was lost and is found, was blind but now can see, was dead and now is alive—this man knows his salvation was not manufactured or self-generated. This salvation came from above; like manna, it is a gift from our merciful Father. And like the heavenly bread which was freely given to the complaining rebels in the wilderness centuries ago, God's benevolent favor descends upon all imperfect, but needy children yet today.

There is never an earthly moment—from spiritual conception and regeneration to our parting breath—that the follower of the Lord Jesus can take credit for anything. Everything we have is a gift; everything has been received. We simply open our hands.

While man does not remain passive in receiving God's grace, he knows even the ability to receive is a gift from God. It is all of grace; hence, there is no room for boasting.

It is so easy for us to forget this. We are naturally prone to pride, self-adulation, and self-preoccupation. We tend to be fiercely independent, often falling into the trap of self-reformation. But only a broken and contrite heart makes room for grace, stripping us of our self-absorption and self-righteousness.

We are well-informed about initial salvation being of grace; we are not so sure about sanctification—God's process of conforming believers to the likeness of Christ. It is one of Satan's deceptive tactics to get us Christians to think that what was initially received by grace can now be perfected by self-effort. If this were so, then there would be grounds for boasting. But it's not so.

The growing, maturing believer learns, and is often reminded, that he is wholly dependent upon the God of all grace in all things, for all things, all the time, and for all time. Every morsel of this heavenly manna is a gift to the undeserving.

Grace be with you!

Come Near to God

[19]Therefore, brothers, since we have confidence to enter the holy places by the blood of Jesus, [20]by the new and living way that he opened for us through the curtain, that is, through his flesh, [21]and since we have a great priest over the house of God, [22]let us draw near with a true heart in full assurance of faith, with our hearts sprinkled clean from an evil conscience and our bodies washed with pure water.
— Hebrews 10:19-22

Come near to God.
How can that be?
I've sinned,
the Law I've broken—
there's no hope for me.

Come near to God.
The way is now open:
Jesus has died,
the Lord crucified—
the veil has been torn.

Come near to God.
With a heart sincere,
Faith fully assured
and heart made clean—
the conscience now clear.

Come near to God.
Your Priest intercedes,
Your Father's arms open,
Your need brings you near—
The Spirit with you pleads.

The Struggle

In your struggle against sin you have not yet resisted to the point of shedding your blood.
— Hebrews 12:4

Devotional writers who suggest there should not be any *struggle* in the life of the Christian, evidently misunderstand what the Bible has to say about the matter.

While the biblical concept of "struggle" is much broader than the occurrences of the word itself (or its synonyms), the contexts in which this word is found in the New Testament reveals the kinds of struggles a Christian does (should?) experience. The Greek word *agōna* (and its derivatives) is variously rendered: race, agony, struggle, fight, conflict (and more). Let's note four kinds of struggle mentioned in the New Testament.

The struggle of an endurance race. Interestingly enough, the Greek word for "race" in Hebrews 12:1, NIV is *agōna:* "Therefore, since we are surrounded by so great a cloud of witnesses, let us also lay aside every weight, and sin which clings so closely, and let us run with endurance the **race** that is set before us . . ."

From beginning to end, this race—this endurance run for the believer—is a conflict against the world, the flesh, and the Devil. There is no better treatise on this subject outside biblical literature than Bunyan's *The Pilgrim Progress*.

The struggle of intercessory prayer. Jesus knew this struggle as no one else as he prayed in Gethsemane: "And being in **agony** he prayed more earnestly, and his sweat became like drops of blood falling down to the ground" (Luke 22:44). Paul references one of his companions in the gospel who experienced the struggle of intercessory prayer: "Epaphras, who is one of you, a servant of Christ Jesus, greets you, always **struggling** on your behalf in his prayers, that you may stand mature and fully assured in all the will of God" (Col. 4:12). Prayer is often a struggle.

The struggle against sin. Because of the benefits flowing from the Cross and the indwelling Spirit, we experience a peace and joy that accompanies a fully surrendered life to the Lord Jesus Christ. However, there remains a struggle, a fight against sin. Hebrews notes: "In your **struggle** against sin you have not yet resisted to the point of shedding your blood" (Hebrews 12:4). To fight against temptation is to struggle against sin. This struggle won't cease until death takes us or until the last trumpet sounds.

The good struggle. Our merciful Father has done for us through Christ, and does for us by his Spirit, all that is necessary for us to win in this struggle. By God's grace, may we be able to say with the holy apostle at the end of our earthly sojourn, "I have **fought** the good **fight** . . ." (2 Tim. 4:7). In the words of Isaac Watts: "Sure, I must fight if I would reign. / Increase my courage, Lord."[13]

The Convert

driven
beaten
barren
fallen

empty
earthy
filthy
guilty

aimless
lifeless
loveless
restless

hollow
shallow
wallow
fallow

sickly
lamely
vainly
darkly

jaded
faded
hated
tainted

striving
vying
sighing
dying

searching
seeking
panting
longing

SAVIOR!
CHANGER!
MASTER!
KEEPER!

smitten
woken
hearken
broken

sinful
awful
woeful
mournful

dawning
bowing
trusting
living

hearing
seeing
rising
walking

joyful
peaceful
hopeful
faithful

changing
praying
praising
gazing

knowing
growing
loving
serving

Evangelical Conversion

. . . you turned to God from idols to serve
the living and true God . . .
— 1 Thessalonians 1:9

Implicit in every genuine conversion to Christ is immediate *change*—a change of attitudes, priorities, principles, lifestyle—a change of heart, mind, and behavior.

The degree of *observable* change depends on how long the new convert has walked in sin, as well as how deep in sin he or she has gone. But let us make no mistake—such a change is observable to all who have known the convert. Many more changes will come and continue to occur throughout the disciple's spiritual pilgrimage, but some degree of immediate change is indigenous to each conversion.

Note three representative biblical witnesses regarding immediate change in the new believer's behavior:

> *And Zacchaeus stood and said to the Lord, "Behold, Lord, the half of my goods I give to the poor. And if I have defrauded anyone of anything, I restore it fourfold"* (Lk 19.8).

> *And he [newly converted jailor] took them the same hour of the night and washed their wounds . . .* (Acts 16:33).

> *. . . you turned to God from idols to serve the living and true*

God . . . (1 Thess. 1:9).

While not all conversions are noticeably dramatic, here is an example of one which was. Before Sam Jones (1847-1906) was converted and became an effective evangelist in Christ's kingdom through the Methodist Church, he lived a deep life of sin. Of the week of his conversion, he says,

> I went to the bar and begged for a glass of liquor. I got the glass and started to drink and looked into the mirror. I saw my hair matted, the filth and vomit on my clothes, one of my eyes totally closed, and my lips swollen. And I said, 'Is that all that is left of the proud and brilliant lawyer, Sam Jones?' I smashed the glass on the floor and fell to my knees and cried, "Oh God! Oh God, have mercy!" The bartender ran to my side and thought I was dying . . . and I was. I said, "Just let me alone." I picked myself up and staggered to my cheap rooming house and said to the ladies running it, "Would you do me a favor?" They answered in the affirmative. I asked them to bring me a pot of black coffee. I went through three days and nights of hell, but when the morning came, something had happened to old Sam Jones. I went down to the clothing store and said, "I want you to give me a new suit. I got saved last night."[14]

Not all converts to Christ were drunkards like Sam Jones, but all genuine converts to Christ are *changed*—and *changing*—disciples of Christ.

Living Stones

[4]As you come to him, a living stone rejected by men but in the sight of God chosen and precious, [5]you yourselves like living stones are being built up a spiritual house, to be a holy priesthood, to offer spiritual sacrifices acceptable to God through Jesus Christ.
— 1 Peter 2:4-5

This world is a great sculptor's shop.
We are the statues and there is a rumor going round the shop that some of us are some day going to come to life.[15]
— C. S. Lewis

A room filled with statues:
all uniquely beautiful,
chiseled and hammered,
made out of stone.

There were ears and eyes,
hands and feet.
But they had no sight;
they did not feel or walk.

They were cold and lifeless stones;
they could not respond.
Void of love and devotion,
they stared, merely stared.

Then without notice
there came a gentle Wind blowing.
The stones became warm;
they could now hear and see.

Walking out of the room
into the loving embrace
of their Sculptor,
they cried, "Father!"

A Confession at 25,000 Feet

". . . but whoever drinks of the water that I will give him will never be thirsty forever."
— John 4:14

Some time ago I was on an airplane flying to the east coast. After boarding the plane, I discovered someone was sitting in my reserved seat. Asking the flight attendant what I should do, he suggested if I wanted to I could take the front row aisle seat. I was happy to do this since it had more leg room.

Since I had a considerable amount of reading I needed to do, I read for the first half of the two-and-a-half hour flight. Finally tiring of reading, I looked up and greeted the attendant, who was seated facing me in the jump seat, six feet away. He warmly acknowledged my greeting, and we began an extended conversation that lasted until the plane touched down.

The man clearly had a story he felt compelled to tell—even to a stranger. Having been an executive for over thirty years with a distinguished company, as well as being a leader in his community, he had been fired from his position. Six months prior to our encounter, he launched a new career as a flight attendant.

Why the firing? He began to rapidly disclose a sordid sexual affair he had engaged in for a number of years with a female co-worker. Finally coming to his senses, he decided he wanted his wife and child more than his paramour, and abruptly broke off the affair. Now embittered, his ex-lover charted a course to make his life miserable. John (not his real name) decided he should tell his superior about the affair before she did, and he lost his job as a result.

Periodically throughout his narrative, John would interject: "I can't believe I'm telling you this; there must be a reason. I never talk like this."

I asked, "John, where are you on your spiritual journey?"

His answer: "I'm Jewish."

"Are you an observant Jew?" I asked.

"No, not really. I never attend synagogue; I never go to worship."

"After realizing the immoral relationship you were in, John, and apologizing to your wife and daughter, did you sense a deeper need of forgiveness—from God?"

"I need to think about that."

"Since you no longer have a Temple where sacrificial offerings are made, and Yeshua—your promised Messiah has come and offered himself as our only atoning sacrifice—you can now be forgiven of all of your sins, you know. I pray that you will."

"Thanks, Ralph; I'll think about that. Do you have a business card?"

With at least four other people within hearing distance of this one hour conversation, I knew why seat 4C had been taken.

The Passage

From . . .

Satan to Christ

in Adam to in Christ

self-righteousness to Christ's righteousness

guilty to blameless

flesh to Spirit

death to life

darkness to light

lost to found

blindness to sight

hate to love

bondage to freedom

fear to faith

self-rule to God's rule

searching to finding

foolishness to wisdom

thirsting to drinking

doubting to knowing

despair to hope

gloom to joy

perishing to living

evil to good

deafness to hearing

filth to purity

ingratitude to thanksgiving

error to truth

torment to peace

anxiety to security

selfishness to service

downward to upward

Conversion

"Go home to your friends and tell them how much the Lord has done for you, and how he has had mercy on you."
— Mark 5:19

Christian conversion is an event as well as a process. By "event," we mean there is a point in time when one is regenerated by the Spirit of God and justified by faith. By "process," we mean one continues to change (sanctification) more and more into the likeness of Christ as he and she grows in the grace and knowledge of God.

The Man from Gadara (see following poem) is a case in point of a conversion event. Prior to his conversion to Christ, this man lived in a cemetery, was inhabited by an unclean spirit, violent and mean, impossible to reason with, and abused his own body. Upon encountering Jesus, he fell at his feet and Jesus cleansed him of his moral impurity and cast the demons from him. There was an immediate observable change to all who witnessed this event: "And they came to Jesus and saw the demon-possessed man, the one who had had the legion, sitting there, clothed and in his right mind, and they were afraid" (Mk 5:15).

While every Christian does not have—nor is expected to have—the kind of dramatic conversion that the Gadarene did, nonetheless, according to God's Word, all who are "in Christ Jesus" have been changed (the Book of Acts and Paul's Epistles are replete with supporting witnesses). To quote one text: "[9]Or do you not know that the unrighteous will not inherit the kingdom of God? Do not be deceived: neither the sexually immoral, nor idolaters, nor adulterers, nor men who practice homosexuality, [10]nor thieves, nor the greedy, nor drunkards, nor revilers, nor swindlers will inherit the kingdom of God. [11]And such were some of you. But you were washed, you were sanctified, you were justified in the name of the Lord Jesus Christ and by the Spirit of our God" (1 Cor. 6:9-11).

But all change does not occur when one is born from above. To these same Corinthians Paul later wrote, "And we all, with unveiled face, beholding the glory of the Lord, are being transformed into the same image [the image of Christ] from one degree of glory to another" (2 Cor. 3:18). Spiritual transformation is an ongoing process—or should be—in the life of every disciple of the Lord Jesus. Our likeness to Jesus will only be *approximated* in this life. However, the New Testament writers expected a growing resemblance to Christ to appear in their converts.

While there are some genuine Christians who cannot point to a conversion event when they came to faith in Christ (having come to Christ at a very young age), the *conscious event* is the biblical norm. For all those who are "in Christ," the challenge is to become more like Christ. This can only occur through a moment-by-moment loving obedience in the Spirit's power.

The Man from Gadara

I despaired of life and living;
All hopes and dreams were gone.
My own sins were all-consuming;
I was the Devil's pawn.

Driven by uncontrolled passion,
Day and night filled with shame;
Slowly my conscience did harden,
Till I lived without aim.

Taking no thought of tomorrow,
The moment was enough.
I tried to avoid all sorrow,
Yet all my days were rough.

I wondered occasionally
As my heart filled with pain,
"Am I to exist slavishly;
Is all my life but vain?"

Then about Jesus they told me,
How he could make me clean;
That he loved the sick and lowly,
That he could change the mean.

I didn't need more information,
This Jesus I must find.
Done was I with hesitation—
Could there be one so kind?

That day I saw Jesus clearly;
At his feet I did fall.
He cast ev'ry demon from me;
He is Lord over all.

Jesus told me to tell my friends
All that he did for me—
How he forgave me all my sins,
Bestowing God's mercy.

This I did to all's amazement,
Preaching Jesus daily;
Telling of his great salvation—
Saving a wretch like me.

I shall never cease to wonder
Why Jesus came my way;
Why he changed my life completely,
Washing my sins away.

The Speaking Word

Mark 5:1-8; 18-20, NKJV

1 Then they came to the other side of the sea, to the country of
the Gadarenes. 2 And when He had come out of the boat, imme-
diately there met Him out of the tombs a man with an unclean
spirit, 3 who had his dwelling among the tombs; and no one
could bind him, not even with chains, 4 because he had often
been bound with shackles and chains. And the chains had been
pulled apart by him, and the shackles broken in pieces; neither
could anyone tame him. 5 And always, night and day, he was in
the mountains and in the tombs, crying out and cutting himself
with stones.

6 When he saw Jesus from afar, he ran and worshiped Him.
7 And he cried out with a loud voice and said, "What have I to
do with You, Jesus, Son of the Most High God? I implore You
by God that You do not torment me." 8 For He said to him,
"Come out of the man, unclean spirit!"

- -

18 And when He got into the boat, he who had been demon-
possessed begged Him that he might be with Him. 19 However,
Jesus did not permit him, but said to him, "Go home to your
friends, and tell them what great things the Lord has done for
you, and how He has had compassion on you." 20 And he de-
parted and began to proclaim in Decapolis all that Jesus had
done for him; and all marveled."

The Carpenter's Yoke

He stumbled into the Carpenter's
shop many years ago,
Longing for the right device
to help him with his load.

Short of breath and bowed down low,
he told about his burden;
Describing as best he knew how
the problem of his condition.

The Carpenter listened compassionately,
as the boy poured forth his plight:
How difficult it was to walk,
though he walked with all his might.

"Could it be," the boy inquired,
"there's something you could make
To help me with this heavy load,
lest under this load I break?"

The kindly Carpenter turned to a rack,
from which he took a yoke—
A device he had skillfully made
with loving hands, stroke by stroke.

With hands controlled by wisdom and love,
he gently lowered the wood,
Until the yoke was firmly set
On the neck of the weary lad.

Looking up with a radiant face,
the boy joyfully exclaimed,
"No longer am I now weighed down;
my load has suddenly drained!"

With a knowing smile and a kindly word,
the Carpenter simply said,
"The yoke I make is easy to wear;
go your way and be glad."

Walking away from the shop that day,
the boy was deep in thought—
"I wonder if it's the scars I saw
that make this *Carpenter different?"*

The Speaking Word

Matthew 11:28-30

[28] *"Come to me, all who labor and are heavy laden, and I will give you rest.* [29] *Take my yoke upon you, and learn from me, for I am gentle and lowly in heart, and you will find rest for your souls.* [30] *For my yoke is easy, and my burden is light."*

— ESV

[28] *Then Jesus said, "Come to me, all of you who are weary and carry heavy burdens, and I will give you rest.* [29] *Take my yoke upon you. Let me teach you, because I am humble and gentle at heart, and you will find rest for your souls.* [30] *For my yoke is easy to bear, and the burden I give you is light."*

— NLT

[28-30] *"Are you tired? Worn out? Burned out on religion? Come to me. Get away with me and you'll recover your life. I'll show you how to take a real rest. Walk with me and work with me—watch how I do it. Learn the unforced rhythms of grace. I won't lay anything heavy or ill-fitting on you. Keep company with me and you'll learn to live freely and lightly."*

— The Message

Are You a New Creature?

Have you confessed Christ as Lord and Savior?
Have you renounced your wicked ways?
Have you turned from all your idols?
Do you seek to live only for God's praise?

Have you done your best to make right your wrongs?
Have you left all the godless crowd?
Have you turned fully to the Lord?
Are you keeping the promises you vowed?

Have you forgiven all who wronged you?
Do you love those you used to hate?
Have you left the works of darkness?
Does the Spirit your life now regulate?

Have you surrendered to God completely?
Have you left all to follow him?
Does Christ own your total loyalty?
Is your body consecrated to him?

Are you truly a new creature in Christ?
Have all the old things passed away?
Are you living a brand new life?
Is Jesus your first love in every way?

Or are you a Christian in name only,
Still living for self and in sin?
If so, bow before Christ lowly;
He will make you new without and within.

Change

Therefore, if anyone is in Christ, he is a new creation.
The old has passed away; behold, the new has come.
— 2 Corinthians 5:17

Just as there are three tenses of salvation—past, present, and future—(see, for example, Eph. 2:8; 1 Cor. 1:18; 1 Thess. 1:10), so there are three tenses of sanctification. Sanctification in practical terms means *change:* what was once considered common has been set apart for holy purposes; what was once used in the service of sin and self is now sacred.

Past tense sanctification. An example of past tense sanctification is located in 1 Corinthians 6. There the apostle Paul writes that specific people, whose lifestyles are characteristically sinful, will not inherit the kingdom of God: the sexually immoral, idolaters, adulterers, those who practice homosexuality, thieves, the greedy, drunkards, revilers, swindlers. Then he reminds his readers: "And such *were* some of you, but you *were* washed, you *were* sanctified, you *were* justified in the name of the Lord Jesus Christ and by the Spirit of God" (v. 11, italics added).

Present tense sanctification. An example of present tense sanctification is located in 2 Corinthians 3:18. In contrasting the veil which covered the face of Moses in order to hide his brilliant countenance, Paul says of those who are in Christ, "And we all, with unveiled face, beholding the glory of the

Lord, are being transformed into the same image from one degree of glory to another." Paul says in 1 Corinthians 6 that every regenerate person has been changed; he says here that every true believer is *being changed* more and more into the likeness of Jesus.

Future tense sanctification. Complete Christlikeness can only be *approximated* in this life. Knowing this gives no genuine Christian excuses, for every person who knows the realities of 1 Corinthians 6 and 2 Corinthians 3:18, also seeks to live a holy life in the power of the Spirit to the glory of God. But such a person knows himself too well to ever say, "I've arrived; finally I'm like Christ in every respect and to every degree." No, he affirms another reality and confesses with the beloved apostle John: "Beloved, we are God's children now, and what we will be has not yet appeared; but we know that when he appears we *will* be like him, because we shall see him as he is" (1 John 3:2, italics added).

In order to experience the final reality—ultimate change—we must have experienced the first reality—past change—and be experiencing the second reality—present change.

Have you been *changed*? Are you *changing*?

Isaiah's Cleansing & Call

"Behold, this has touched your lips; your iniquity is taken away and your sin is forgiven."
— Isaiah 6:7, NASB

Instinctively I saw the failures in others;
quick was I to judge their sin.
Denouncing the hypocrisies in my brothers,
covered my own lack within.

Then what I depended on was taken from me—
stripped of all self-confidence.
Desperately falling before God Almighty,
there I faced my arrogance.

Seeing the Lord in undiluted holiness,
high and lofty on a throne;
Suddenly I felt the shame of my uncleanness:
pervasive . . . and all of my own.

So overwhelming was my complete defilement,
I wept and wept with much woe.
But then I felt his fire and heard the announcement,
which began with a clear "Lo."

"Lo, this fiery, sacred coal has touched your deep need,
as a sign of your cleansing.
Your iniquity is gone; your sin all atoned."
I knew this was life-changing.

Then I heard the voice of the Lord distinctly ask,
"Who shall represent Us?"
Unworthily, I replied—now stripped of my mask—
"Send me; you're now my focus!"

Though called by God to preach his message with passion
to a rebellious people,
I do so today with a heart of compassion,
since that Day in the temple.

The Pure in Heart

"Blessed are the pure in heart, for they shall see God."
— Matthew 5:8

The pure in heart have been to the holy mount and have gazed upon the face of the exact representation of God, the Lord Jesus Christ. They behold not only the Jesus of history, they contemplate the living Christ of eternity—the Christ who said, "I am . . . the Living One; I was dead, and behold I am alive for ever and ever!" (Rev. 1:18, NIV).

The pure in heart have seen God. Not in his full revelation, but in Jesus. "Whoever has seen me has seen the Father" (John 14:9). To see God is not to see God with the physical eye, but to see God with the eye of faith. "Though you have not seen him, you love him; though you do not see him, you believe in him and rejoice with joy that is inexpressible and filled with glory . . ." (1 Pet. 1:8).

The pure in heart have seen a God who is glorious in holiness ("in him is no darkness at all," 1 Jo. 1:5). God's holiness is absolute. That is why neither man nor beast were permitted to touch Mount Sinai when the Law was given. Only Moses and Joshua were allowed to ascend the mountain—men who had consecrated themselves wholly to God and who had been made holy by God (see Ex. 19).

The pure in heart wills one thing—they will the will of God.

However imperfectly they may perform that will, however far short they fall in resembling the Lord Jesus Christ—nevertheless, they will to do the will of God.

The pure in heart are more conscious of their own shortcomings, failures in performing the will of God perfectly, and unlikeness to the Lord Jesus Christ—more than anyone else. They habitually confess their need for God's holiness. They know apart from Christ they are altogether sinful and unclean.

The pure in heart have experienced a deeper and deepening purity of heart through a grace that has enabled them to obey God more completely. The language of their spirit is, "Yes, Lord." Peter and the Apostles knew this well; so did Cornelius and his household. "[The Holy Spirit] made no distinction between us and them, having cleansed their hearts by faith" (Acts 15:9).

Why do learned minds argue whether God can purify one's heart in this world?

"Blessed are the pure in heart, for they shall see God" (Mt. 5:8).

Noble Vessels

In every large and wealthy household
the kitchen is a place to behold;
Vessels fill the shelves from every mold:
wood, earthenware, some silver, some gold.

Some of these vessels are quite noble,
chosen for work that is notable—
Strong, solid and very durable,
their service is most invaluable.

Other vessels are cheap, average;
these don't serve well as they grow in age.
The master finds these hard to manage,
so in time they have no more usage.

Each Christian must make a decision—
which vessel will fill all his vision.
Will the lowest be his conclusion,
or will the highest claim his mission?

How might I a noble vessel be,
one serving my Master faithfully?
Cleanse myself from all that's unworthy;
then he can use me when he's ready.

A Vessel for Noble Purposes

[20]In a large house there are articles not only of gold and silver, but also of wood and clay; some are for noble purposes and some for ignoble. [21]If a man cleanses himself from the latter, he will be an instrument for noble purposes, made holy, useful to the Master and prepared to do any good work.
— 2 Timothy 2:20-21, NIV

After many years of carefully observing the ways of God with the children of men, the venerable John Wesley (1703-1791) wrote:

> From long experience and observation, I am inclined to think that whoever finds redemption in the blood of Jesus—whoever is justified—has the choice of walking in the higher or lower path. I believe the Holy Spirit at that time sets before him the "more excellent way" and cites him to walk therein—to choose the narrowest path in the narrow way—to aspire after the heights and depths of holiness—after the entire image of God. But if he does not accept this offer, he insensibly declines into the lower order of Christians; he still goes on in what may be called a good way, serving God in his degree, and finds mercy in the close of life through the blood of the covenant.[16]

Methodism's founder was simply reiterating in his own words the same truth affirmed in the Scripture above. The church of the Lord Jesus Christ consists of two categories of believers: the "vessels for ignoble purposes" and the "vessels for noble purposes." The ignoble are likened to wood and clay; the noble resemble the precious metals of gold and silver.

The apostle informs us that the ignoble vessels can become noble if they so choose. But there is a price to pay. If the ignoble vessel becomes totally dissatisfied with his lowly condition, he must take resolute, radical measures in order to change his status; he must rid himself of all the "wood" and "clay" in his life.

Sadly, the church is populated with too many ignoble vessels. Who among us will hear the voice of the Spirit calling us to a noble life, a holy life? Who will cleanse himself from all that contaminates the body and spirit? Who will consecrate himself totally to the Lord? Who will aspire to be a noble vessel to the glory and praise of the Lord Jesus? Only noble vessels are fully useful vessels—useful according to God's standard of usefulness.

Dear reader, will you aspire to be a vessel for noble purposes? Would you be willing to cleanse yourself—by the enabling grace of God—from everything in your life that is "wood and clay"?

God is wanting to make you and me into "gold and silver" vessels.

Like a Grain of Wheat

As lovely as it may be to the eyes,
a lone grain is worthless unless it dies;
But if it falls hidden into the ground,
from death eventually it will abound.

To save myself is but to lose my life—
self-sovereignty is a kingdom of grief.
But to lose myself is to gain with God,
and to take the path that Jesus trod.

Our Lord led the way by the death he died;
surrendered fully, he was crucified.
What seemed that Day to be a tragic loss,
was in fact total triumph through the Cross.

If I am to live life to the fullest,
wanting to see an abundant harvest,
Like him I must fall like a grain of wheat—
into the ground before the Mercy Seat.

Renouncing my prideful, self-centered way,
in full surrender I sign my life away.
Entrusting to him my past and future;
rising from the ground in the Spirit's pow'r.

The Speaking Word

As lovely as it may be to the eyes . . .

"Truly, truly, I say to you, unless a grain of wheat falls into the earth and dies, it remains alone; but if it dies, it bears much fruit."

— John 12:24

To save myself is but to lose my life . . .

"Whoever loves his life loses it, and whoever hates his life in this world will keep it for eternal life."

— John 12:25

Our Lord led the way by the death he died . . .

For to this you have been called, because Christ also suffered for you, leaving you an example, so that you might follow in his steps.

— 1 Peter 2:21

If I am to live life to the fullest . . .

"I came that they may have life and have it abundantly."

— John 10:10

The power is his, I am ever mindful . . .

"I am the vine; you are the branches. Whoever abides in me and I in him, he it is that bears much fruit, for apart from me you can do nothing."

— John 15:5

Renouncing my prideful, self-centered way . . .

Then Jesus told his disciples, "If anyone would come after me, let him deny himself and take up his cross and follow me."

— Matthew 16:24

A Treasure Rare

Christ in you, the hope of glory.
— Colossians 1:27, NASB

That which hinders and slackens a winning pace,
every impediment in this race;
Each contaminant spoiling the soul,
whatever keeps from making me whole—
These weights to the Cross, O Lord, I bring,
presenting my body as an offering.

Leaving my sinful self and choice idols there,
I find fresh life and a Treasure rare.
This precious Treasure is Christ in me,
granted to those seeking thirstily—
Those who are desperate in their faith,
this Treasure gives unimaginable strength.

What once I attempted in futility
has become a blest reality;
Instead of trying to be better,
this inner Guest is now my Victor.
Christ in me—an abiding Treasure—
fills my days and my nights with joyful pleasure.

The power is his, I am ever mindful,
knowing my vessel is but fragile.
I pray, O Lord, for your constant care,
Christ in me!—I stand guard jealously—
lest lesser loves come steal this Treasure from me.

Sin is Still *Sin*

Yet if it had not been for the law, I would not have known sin.
— Romans 7:7

When American psychiatrist Dr. Karl Menninger published his book *Whatever Became of Sin?* in 1973, it shook the medical/psychological establishment. The reason it sent shock waves throughout the halls of academia is contained in the book's very title. Menninger was not willing to write off *every* disease, perversity, obsession, addiction, and so on, as simply a mental disorder or social malfunction.

Though not a trained theologian, Menninger did a better job at defining sin than many ministers and seminary professors do. He said, "sin is any behavior that violates the moral code or the individual conscience or both; behavior which pains or harms or destroys my neighbor—or me, myself." Further, he says, sin "is a willful, defiant, or disloyal quality; someone is defiled or offended or hurt. The willful disregard or sacrifice of the welfare of others for the welfare of the self is an essential quality of the concept of sin . . ."[17]

Menninger's definition of sin is very close to the Bible's own definition and description of sin. Referring to his preconversion conviction of sin, the apostle Paul wrote, "Yet if it had not been for the law, I would not have known sin. I would not have known what it is to covet if the law had not said, 'You shall not covet'" (Rom. 7:7), a reference to God's moral code, the Ten Commandments. Paul said there was a time when he felt no guilt, shame or conviction for doing sinful things. Why? "Apart from the law [the law of God] sin lies dead." Then he says, "I was once alive apart from the law; but when the commandment came, sin came alive and I died [died to sin]" (Rom. 7:8-9).

A popular TV preacher, who has an audience of millions, was asked why he never mentions sin in his preaching. His reply: "I don't want people to feel bad after they hear me speak. I want them to go away feeling uplifted."

What did Paul write to those who believed one could live any way he wished and still expect to go to Heaven? "Or do you not know that the unrighteous will not inherit the kingdom of God? Do not be deceived: neither the sexually immoral, nor idolaters, nor adulterers, nor men who practice homosexuality,
[10]nor thieves, nor the greedy, nor drunkards, nor revilers, nor swindlers will inherit the kingdom of God. [11]And such *were*
some of you. But you *were* washed, you *were* sanctified, you *were* justified in the name of the Lord Jesus Christ and by the Spirit of our God" (1 Cor. 6:9-11, emphasis added).

When the pulpit is silent where God's Word is vocal, the pew will interpret the silence as permission to engage in activities proscribed by the written Word of God. It is time to again call sin what the Bible calls *sin*.

Christ Reigns Within

The kingdom of God has come to reign,
having conquered my lowly domain.
No more do I want to control my life;
gone is fleshly resistance and strife.
Christ is King of my heart and my soul;
to him I've given total control.
Christ reigns within!

Once with great fear my mind debated;
the King's demands I contemplated:
Self-surrender without condition,
full allegiance of my volition,
To sacrifice my idol dearest,
pledge my passions to all that's purest.
Christ reigns within!

A kingdom of righteousness and love
has marched in with my King from above;
Overthrowing every native foe,
breaking down heavily entrenched woe.
His campaign perseveres without end,
taking forces reluctant to bend.
Christ reigns within!

The kingdom of God has come inside;
my heart, the King, has come to reside.
The standard he's raised is holiness;
his Name will settle for nothing less.
With merciful grace he shapes my will,
breathing his power in me to fill.
Christ reigns within!

The Speaking Word

The kingdom of God has come to reign . . .

"Your kingdom come, your will be done, on earth as it is in heaven."

— Matthew 6:10

Once with great fear my mind debated . . .

"No one can serve two masters, for either he will hate the one and love the other, or he will be devoted to the one and despise the other."

— Matthew 6:24

A kingdom of righteousness and love . . .

For the kingdom of God is not a matter of eating and drinking but of righteousness and peace and joy in the Holy Spirit.

— Romans 14:17

The kingdom of God has come inside . . .

Now when He was asked by the Pharisees when the kingdom of God would come, He answered them and said, "The kingdom of God does not come with observation; nor will they say, 'See here!' or 'See there!' For indeed, the kingdom of God is within you."

— Luke 17:20-21, NKJV

The Son of Man

It mattered not the circumstance—
friendly or a foreboding Providence—
Our Master enjoyed fellowship
and Father's unbroken companionship.
He was the worshiping *Son of Man.*

Not starting a task on his own
before his Father's purpose was first known;
He often spent time on a hill
alone, discovering his Father's will.
He was the praying *Son of Man.*

When he walked on earth as a man,
the Lord Jesus worked according to plan—
Whether plying fresh wood with tools,
or repairing a yoke for farmers' bulls.
He was the laboring *Son of Man.*

Often seen touching the unclean,
and driving demons from the possessed mean;
He wept when his dear friend had died,
and acted when a poor blind man had cried.
He was the caring *Son of Man.*

For sinners, he died once for all;
then arose, defeating Adam's deep fall;
Ascended to resounding praise,
now preparing his spotless Bride a place.
He is the coming *Son of Man.*

Work & Worship

. . . work with your hands, as we instructed you . . .
— 1 Thessalonians 4:11

"God is spirit, and those who worship him must worship in spirit and truth."
— John 4:24

Man was created to work and worship. Regrettably, the church knows far more about the former than it does the latter. Such an imbalance is reflected by my desk dictionary. *The American Heritage Dictionary of the English Language* (4th edition) takes 118 lines to define "work" while only using 11 lines to define "worship." (Of course, the dictionary is rarely a helpful resource in defining and describing spiritual realities.) Could it be that the same ratio exists in the church as it does in this dictionary—118:11?

I recently heard a pastor relate that when he suggested in a church business meeting that the matter under discussion should be given earnest prayer before a decision was made, a prominent deacon retorted: "This is a business meeting, not a prayer meeting!" The autopsy report on such a church might read: "Deadsville Church expired because it elected spiritually unqualified leaders who knew more about *business* than they did about God."

How different from the above was the reputation of one English deacon. Before he became a renowned preacher and

Bible conference teacher, Dr. J. Sidlow Baxter (1903-199) was the pastor of Bethesda Free Church in Sunderland, County Durham, England. He recalls the following: "I began to hear many appreciative remarks concerning a former deacon who had died a few years earlier. I was told it was almost impossible to think or speak unworthily in his presence; that he always brought a sense of God's presence when he came into a room; and that in the office bearers' meetings, if a discussion ever seemed to be getting edgy or uncharitable, he would quietly rise and lead the brethren in such a prayer that afterward the discussion could only continue on a high spiritual plane."[18]

Who was that deacon? William D. Longstaff (1822-1894), author of one of the church's beautiful hymns of devotion—"Take Time to Be Holy." Four lines of Longstaff's poem read:

Take time to be holy,
Speak oft with thy Lord
Abide in Him always,
And feed on His word.[19]

The church is called to work and worship. To engage in activities—even worthy ones—without a sense of God-consciousness, is but "sound and fury signifying nothing." We can only give cups of water in Jesus' name if we have first bent low to worship. Such soul-posture would transfigure even the church's business meetings.

The Temple of Christ

You have overthrown the tables
Of wickedness and rebellion.
Ev'ry idol I thought hidden,
You've driv'n from a will once stubborn.

You have come into your temple;
You have removed all corruption.
You have taken up residence,
To live without interruption.

Where once there was desecration,
Your holiness has since displaced.
Where self had lived as your rival,
Your presence everywhere is graced.

My body's now your sacred temple,
Reserved for only you to dwell;
All members fully surrendered,
To the blessed Immanuel.

In this holy habitation
Let constant hallelujahs rise,
Since Christ the mighty Conqueror
Fills the temple where he abides.

God's Dwelling Place

Or do you not know that your body is a temple of the Holy Spirit within you, whom you have from God?
— 1 Corinthians 6:19

That the Lord God should choose to dwell in man is utterly incomprehensible. That he who is high and lofty, holy and infinite, perfect in all he is and does—that such a God should bend to inhabit fallen man must make even angels wonder.

Where God dwells there is inevitable disruption. No less disturbing is his arrival in a sinful soul than it was the day when the Lord Jesus, walking into the Temple overthrew tables of greed and covetousness, driving from that consecrated place all wickedness and selfishness.

The city of Corinth was notorious for sexual impurities. It was a city of 12 temples. One of the most infamous of these was dedicated to Aphrodite, the goddess of love, whose worshipers practiced religious prostitution. At one time 1,000 prostitutes served in this temple. Sexual immorality was so rampant in Corinth that the Greek verb "to Corinthianize" came to mean "to practice sexual immorality."

We also live in a day when sexual immorality is pervasive. No popular medium of communication is exempt from Satan's evil creations and devices to lure the curiosities of God's people to explore the impure and licentious. The printed page, television, the Internet, and videos, are all being exploited by our Adversary to destroy the love and faith of God's people.

How are we to respond to this *Niagara* of sexual depravity?

- *Consecrate* our body to the Lord Jesus Christ (Rom. 12:1).

- *Remember* that such property—our body—is the sacred temple of the Lord Jesus Christ, in which he dwells (1 Cor. 6:19).

- *Seek daily* to walk in the Spirit so as not to engage in the acts of the flesh (Gal. 5:16).

- *Remember* at what cost we were purchased and that we are Another's property (1 Cor. 6:20).

- *Habitually* honor God with our body (1 Cor. 6:20).

Our body . . . God's dwelling place! What God expects from us, his Spirit will enable our wills to perform.

What to Pray

That for which I had fervently prayed,
thinking I knew what was best,
My loving, wise heavenly Father
chose to deny my request.

Time and again I petitioned him,
knowing his love was steadfast;
Surely he would give this to his child,
since his power was so vast.

With many tears and an aching heart,
I made my petition known;
I prayed on in faith day after day
before a merciful throne.

Then one dark night in anguish of soul
I heard a voice speak clearly;
Immediately I stopped asking—
instead—listened intently.

"I never withhold from my children,
what I know is for their good;
Trust in me as your all-wise Father,
and only pray as you should.

Listen once again to how my Son
taught my children what to say.
Always pray, 'Thy will be done'—
this I'll answer every day."

On that night I learned a great lesson,
that will never go away—
When praying to my all-wise Father,
what I must now always say.

Your Will be Done

"Your will be done on earth as it is in heaven."
— Matthew 6:10, NKJV

That God has a *will*, and that the disciple of the Lord Jesus is to always pray in harmony with our Lord's will, is a teaching clearly taught in the sacred Scriptures.

John tells us, "And this is the confidence that we have toward him, that if we ask anything according to his will he hears us. [15]And if we know that he hears us in whatever we ask, we know that we have the requests that we have asked of him" (1 John 5:14-15). The Lord Jesus instructs us to pray, "Your will be done," and he is likewise an example of such, by praying in Gethsemane, "My Father, if it be possible, let this cup pass from me; nevertheless, not as I will, but as you will" (Mt. 26:39).

Since the Bible teaches that it is imperative for the believer to offer his prayers according with the will of God, can we actually know we are offering our petitions in God's will? Yes. If the matter for which we are petitioning God is clearly covered in the Scriptures, then the believer has been supplied through God's written revelation as to what his will is. This is clearly the case in areas of morality and righteousness. For example, if a new believer asks God if he should continue to have a sexual relationship with a person he is not married to, the Bible explicitly addresses this kind of sinful conduct. On the other hand, if a believer asks God if he should resign job "A" to take job "B," the Scriptures will not *tell* the believer what to do, but does furnish him with many "pointers" (principles) in ascertaining God's will in matters of personal guidance.

If as followers of the Lord Jesus we are to *pray* in the will of God, it is essential that we *live* in the will of God. James declared, "The prayer of a righteous man is powerful and effective" (James 5:16, NIV). Only those who are living in a *right relationship* with God—"a righteous man"—can offer prayers in the will of God.

If we do not know how to pray about a particular matter, we can at least *groan*: "For we do not know what to pray for as we ought, but the Spirit himself intercedes for us with groaning too deep for words. And he who searches hearts knows what is the mind of the Spirit, because the Spirit intercedes for the saints according to the will of God" (Rom. 8:26-27).

To pray "Your will be done" should not be prayed with an attitude of defeated resignation, but with a joyful surrender and implicit confidence, knowing that our sovereign God and Father *knows* what is best.

Daily Bread

Is it bread I need, day by day?
my Father says merely to ask.
Would he withhold from his own child
what is required to do his task?

How could I not trust my Father,
the One who made the earth and grain,
The One whose Son multiplied loaves
and causes wheat to grow with rain?

In vain I do fret and worry,
wondering how needs shall be met,
When all I have to do is trust
my Father, by whose strength I'm kept.

Since my ev'ry hair is numbered,
and he sees the sparrow fallen—
He knows my each and ev'ry need,
telling me I'm not forgotten.

My Father is never passive
of what I need for ev'ry day;
But through his own Son, Christ Jesus,
provides the means and makes a way.

Is it bread I need, day by day?
my Father says merely to ask.
Would he withhold from his own child
what is required to do his task?

And when that day will soon arrive
when I don't need my daily bread,
I'll be taken to Christ on high,
still feeding on my living Head.

"Give us this day . . ."

"Give us this day this day our daily bread . . ."
— Matthew 6:11

The Son of God was also very much the Son of Man—a real man. Because he was a man, he experienced the same physical needs of every other human being. He needed air to breathe, water to drink, clothes to wear, shelter to retire to, and food to eat.

During the time of his earthly sojourn, the Lord Jesus expressed the heart of the Father in many ways. One of those ways was the care and compassion he showed toward hungry people—people who were in need of food.

Many Christians who sincerely aspire to live wholly for God, forget in their quest to be Christlike that the Father is vitally interested in the whole person—including the human body. Because God is our Creator and Redeemer, Christians are reminded in the sacred text that the body is the temple of the Holy Spirit, whose members are to be engaged in only what is morally good and acceptable. Neither is a Christian to defile his body or mistreat it in any way. Why? Because it is the Spirit's temple and has (or should be) been totally consecrated to God (see Romans 12:1, 2; 1 Corinthians 6:12-20; Romans 6:15-19).

While God's design for Christians is to live a morally clean life before him, it is also God's design and desire to personally care for the material and bodily needs of his children. As a loving and merciful heavenly Father who created the lilies of the field and sees every fallen sparrow, and who knows us so intimately that the hairs of our head are numbered—this same Father wants to furnish my every material need.

Thus, in addition to teaching us to pray for the complete and universal reign of his kingdom, to pray for his will to rule, to pray for the forgiveness of our trespasses and sins—our Lord also taught us to look to him for our daily material needs.

When Jesus taught his disciples to pray, "Give us this day our daily bread," he inferred not only were they dependent on the Father to meet their needs, but also that the Father would answer such a petition.

While the Father will answer this petition of his children in a variety of ways—including giving one the strength and ability to earn bread—be assured, he will answer.

And while the Father is answering our own petition for bread, let us not forget to share that bread, as we are able, with others who are in need.

For These I Ask

Reverence—
for your name most high;
Surrender—
to you instead of I.

Gratitude—
for gifts undeserved;
Forgiveness—
for each debt I've incurred.

Glory—
to you alone giv'n;
Praise—
for your Son in Heaven.

Blessings—
on those to me special;
Conversions—
attending the gospel.

Love—
for you totally;
Compassion—
in serving the lowly.

Unity—
for all who are thine;
Fruitfulness—
for each branch on the Vine.

Servants—
your fire make holy;
Grace—
to proclaim Christ boldly.

Faith—
when doubt attacks near;
Hope—
through every dreadful fear.

Joy—
flowing from our meet;
Peace—
spreading with both my feet.

Insight—
to perceive your word;
Strength—
to apply what I've heard.

Wisdom—
to choose what is right;
Obedience—
walking in all your light.

Thoughtfulness—
in every relation;
Humility—
to know limitation.

Steadfastness—
in life's trials met;
Faithfulness—
with each covenant kept.

Discipline—
to do what I should;
Time—
to do works that are good.

Watchfulness—
lest Satan devours;
Protection—
in all my leisure hours.

Confession—
when for you I've failed;
Recourse—
it's to the Cross I'm nailed.

Brilliant Luminaries

[14]Do all things without grumbling or questioning,
[15]that you may be blameless and innocent, children of God
without blemish in the midst of a crooked and twisted generation,
among whom you shine as lights in the world . . .
— Philippians 2:14-15

The inspired letter writer in describing the moral climate of his own generation, said it was both "crooked and twisted" (Phil. 2:15). They were "crooked" with regard to their behavior, and "twisted" with respect to their mindset. Unlike today's typical philosopher and counselor, Paul believed in a revealed, moral objective standard of thinking and conduct, otherwise such descriptions would be meaningless—behavior and worldviews can't be considered "crooked" and "twisted" unless there is a *straight* and *right* standard of thinking and conduct.

Christians have always lived in a morally depraved and degenerate culture, but it's getting worse. If you question that, read 2 Timothy 3.

But the issue is not how bad the world is; the question for Christians is how are we to live in such a world of moral blight? Staying with the same textual context (Phil. 2:14-15), the first century apostle-teacher exhorted the Philippian believers to counter their fallen culture by walking cautiously and reverentially before God. Such a walk would impact even their speech—a speech that would be characterized by an absence of "complaining," and "questioning." The one speaks of ingratitude, the other of unbelief.

By living such a grace-filled lifestyle, Paul says such believers are blameless before God, morally unadulterated, and walking in such purity that they will look like true children of God. Such transformed individuals stand out. The apostle says they will "shine as lights in the world."

This world is in desperate need of brilliant luminaries. With its crooked and twisted views of everything God has ordained and commanded, the Christian is called to *shine*. We are to shine in our attitudes, speech, and conduct. We are called to live a life of Christlike integrity.

God has not called us to be brazen and inconsiderate. We are not called to be obnoxious and rude. We are called by a holy God to live-out in a dark culture a life that is no less and no more than that of a mere Christian.

It would be easy—the natural thing to do—to be constantly complaining about what's bad in people and our society. God is not pleased with complainers; he has called us to do what his Son did for three years—simply go about doing good.

We don't have to *force* the light. Just be Christian . . . and you'll shine.

Praying for Wisdom

Do you want to know what God wills you to do;
is it for wisdom your heart cries out?
Are you earnestly seeking for Heaven's view;
can God lead his child without a doubt?

The Father invites you to make your request,
to present your need before the throne.
He directs the steps of those who are nearest,
revealing his will to them alone.

When making your request, expect a reply;
don't approach with a mind divided.
Your Father prefers not your request to deny,
but you must not come undecided.

To the one who in mind is vacillating,
doubting if God can show the way,
He need not expect an answer forthcoming,
for such it is quite useless to pray.

True to his Word, God gives wisdom liberally,
to each one asking in faith for it.
He never resents his child asking largely—
the one who is led by his Spirit.

The Speaking Word

James 1:5-8

Do you want to know what God wills you to do . . .
If any of you lacks wisdom . . .

The Father invites you to make your request . . .
. . . let him ask God . . . and it will be given him . . .

When making your request, expect a reply . . .
But let him ask in faith, with no doubting, for the one who doubts is like a wave of the sea that is driven and tossed by the wind.

To the one who in mind is vacillating . . .
For that person must not suppose that he will receive anything from the Lord; he is a double-minded man, unstable in all his ways.

True to his Word, God gives wisdom liberally . . .
. . . who gives generously to all without reproach . . .

Persistent Prayer

He had just retired for the night;
his wife and children were in bed.
There were no lights on in the house;
I approached the door with some dread.

It's true, the hour was quite late;
I was no doubt quite presumptuous.
But a friend had come as a guest;
I hoped my neighbor was gracious.

As soon as I knocked on the door,
I told my neighbor my sad plight:
"I only need three loaves of bread;
a guest has arrived for the night."

He was in no mood to get up,
but I kept knocking just the same.
I needed this food for my friend;
I couldn't return home in shame.

At last, the man opened the door,
with loaves of bread numbering three.
"I don't give these 'cause you're my friend;
it was your persistence, you see."

When Jesus told this parable,
he taught this important lesson:
Never give up making requests;
Father will answer in season.

(Based on Luke 11:5-10.)

Believing Prayer

"Therefore I tell you, whatever you ask in prayer, believe that you have received it, and it will be yours."
— Mark 11:24

At first glance, the title of this meditation may appear redundant. After all, is there such a thing as praying without believing? Surely we need go no further to obtain an honest answer to this question than to make a candid appraisal of our own prayer life (assuming that yours is no different than mine).

How much of our praying is half-hearted—lacking earnestness, passion, fervency and faith? How often do we go to our knees (Does anyone actually kneel anymore?) with the subliminal thought: *Will God actually answer my petition? Is Jesus Christ truly the same yesterday, today, and forever? Is God indeed a rewarder of those who earnestly seek him? Did Jesus really mean, "Everyone who asks, receives"?*

Prior to his conversion to Christ, Charles Finney (1792-1875)—who later was God's instrument in revival in Upstate New York in the 19th century—frequently attended a midweek prayer service in Adams, New York. A young attorney at the time, Finney reports that during one of these services he was asked if he wanted the Christians there to pray for him. In his own words, here is his rather audacious reply: "I suppose I need to be prayed for, for I am conscious I am a sinner; but I do not see that it will do any good for you to pray for me; for you are continually asking, but you do not receive."[20] What an indictment! Happily, later that church's prayer life was transformed as well as Finney's.

In the early part of the 20th century, a 24-year-old Lutheran pastor by the name of Armin Gesswein (1909-2001) was doing his best to plant a new church on Long Island, New York. Things weren't going well for this fledgling minister. Writing about it years later, Gesswein says his ministry was transformed when he began to pray differently.

There was a blacksmith in this little church by the name of Ambrose Whalen. Whalen had the reputation of getting his prayers answered. Desperate for help himself, Gesswein asked Whalen one day if he could join him in prayer. He was invited to the blacksmith's home. Once there, Gesswein says they went to Whalen's barn and climbed to the hayloft. The young pastor prayed first. Then the old blacksmith prayed. After he finished, Gesswein asked, "You have some kind of secret in praying. Would you share it with me?" "Young man," said the blacksmith, "Learn to plead the promises of God."[21]

The old man was kneeling between two bales of hay. On each bale was an open Bible. As he prayed, he prayed believing God meant what he said—each hand on a promise of God.

Prayer: *Lord, transform my prayer life until I will pray with true faith in you. Amen.*

The Truly Happy

The man who does not order his life
on the basis of ungodly advisors,
nor hang out with God-rejecters,
nor has fellowship with the profane—
this man is blessed by God
and is truly happy.

This blessed and truly happy man
gets more excited over the truth
and wisdom of God
than anything else in life.
He delights in God's truth so much
that he ponders it again and again.

Because he takes God and his ways seriously,
this blessed and truly happy man
will become so grounded in God
that he will be abundantly creative and productive.
Even when life is tough and difficult,
God will cause him to flourish.

Conversely, those who reject God and his advice
are without substance and stability;
therefore they will fail the Great Inspection—
their lives were but a sham.
God will not allow them to
coexist with his people in their eternal Home.

The Lord approves of the way
of the truly happy man—
the one he himself blesses—
the one who is God-centered in all he does.
But for those who live without reference to God—
all their dreams and pursuits will go up in flames.

(Paraphrase of Psalm 1)

God's Balance

Inherent in the very character of God is a perfect hatred of evil and a perfect love for righteousness—the one assumes the other. One existing without the other would not be the God, Creator, and Redeemer revealed through both the written and living Word, but a caricature. The Eternal God is beautiful in holiness, because he is perfectly symmetrical in all his attributes and ways. He always acts and reacts in character—because of who he is.

To pursue a life of holiness is to avoid sin and embrace righteousness. It is to have the mind of Christ; it is to imitate God as revealed in the person of his Son through the power of the indwelling Christ.

True Holiness involves a negative and a positive. The earnest follower of the Lord Jesus Christ is characterized by both what he *does* as well as by what he *avoids;* what he *embraces* as well as by what he *shuns.*

Much of contemporary Christianity ignores the description of the balanced believer as recorded in Psalm 1. But it's there just the same. The psalmist says that the truly happy Christian is blessed by God because of what he does as well as by what he doesn't do; the blessed person lives differently from all those surrounding him. And because he lives differently, his everlasting habitation will be different from those who are not blessed by God.

In some Christian circles, one mostly hears the refrain of verse 1:

The man who does not order his life
on the basis of ungodly advisors,
nor hang out with God-rejecters,
nor has fellowship with the profane—
this man is blessed by God
and is truly happy (RIT).

In other Christian circles, the refrain of verse 2 is heard more often:

This blessed and truly happy man
gets more excited over the truth
and wisdom of God
than anything else in life.
He delights in God's truth so much
that he ponders it again and again (RIT).

The blessed person learns to embrace both truths.

Prayer: *Lord Jesus, by the presence and power of your indwelling Spirit, shape me into the kind of person who resembles you—the one who was anointed with joy because he hated iniquity. Amen.*

Models of Faith

They were plain people, not unlike you and me,
Who to the call of God responded
With an innermost born conviction
That his revealed Word could be trusted—
Regardless of their present situation.
They are models of faith.

Their respective tasks and exploits were unique,
As each one's gifts and temperament.
But in this they were all just the same:
Each saw that God was omnipotent—
And walked steadfastly before him without blame.
They are models of faith.

To these men and women of deep piety,
Faith was a living reality,
Compelling them to live uprightly,
Rejecting all popularity—
Learning to embrace God's truth wholeheartedly.
They are models of faith.

Whether offering a better sacrifice,
Or preparing to escape a flood,
Forsaking home for another land,
Or being rescued by a lamb's blood—
These faithful were guided by an unseen hand.
They are models of faith.

But not all were delivered from difficulties.
Some in deserts all lonely wandered;
Others wore goatskins for their clothing.
Some were afflicted and ill-treated—
Others chose death over compromising.
They are models of faith.

Surrounded as we are by such witnesses,
Let us put off every encumbrance
And that which so easily trips us,
Running this race with all endurance—
Let us gaze with steadfast eyes upon Jesus.
He's our perfecter of faith.

(Based on Hebrews 11:1-12:1:2.)

The Thirsty

[37]On the last day of the feast, the great day, Jesus stood up and cried out, "If anyone thirsts, let him come to me and drink. [38]Whoever believes in me, as the Scripture has said, 'Out of his heart will flow rivers of living water.'"
— John 7:37-38

Water has always been a precious natural resource. Whenever a severe hurricane or earthquake strikes, cutting off the affected area's power supply, one of the first calls for help is for water.

All plant and animal life depend on water for their daily sustenance. Where there is no water there is no life. One can travel for hundreds of miles through desert wasteland without a sign of life because of the absence of water; when the signs of life appear, there is sure to be the presence of water.

Water is used in the Scriptures as a symbol of the essential life-giving sustenance of God. Jesus said that he himself was the source and fountainhead of spiritual life (see Rev. 21:6). Without Christ we live in a desert; with Christ we enjoy an eternal oasis.

Some of God's final words of written revelation are in the form of an invitation—an invitation offered to the thirsty and desiring: "And let the one who is thirsty come; let the one who desires take the water of life without price" (Rev. 22:17). Here, "desires" is used to underscore with intensity the appetite of "the one who is thirsty." Both "thirsty " and "desires" are present participles, which should culminate in deliberate, decisive action—"take" (aorist tense).

Spiritual thirst and desire are Spirit-induced, not self-induced. Spiritual desire comes from God and must be acted upon with a decisive will, empowered by grace. Where spiritual desire fails to be acted upon, our spirit is left depleted and unfulfilled. When our desire for God finds its satisfaction in him—taking the water of life—our spirit is refreshed, renewed, and satisfied.

The Lord Jesus is both the source and object of such thirst. We drink from him—and are satisfied. He is our salvation—we are satisfied; he is our life—we keep on drinking. "To have found God and still to pursue Him is the soul's paradox of love,"[22] observed A. W. Tozer. Every God-thirsty Christian is a witness to such reality.

In the timeless words of Bernard of Clairvaux (1090-1153):

We taste Thee, O Thou Living Bread,
  And long to feast upon Thee still:
We drink of Thee, the Fountainhead
  And thirst our souls from Thee to fill.[23]

Things Above

Since I have been raised up with Christ my Lord,
all things above I am seeking;
Things which can be found where only Christ is,
at God's right hand interceding.

On things above I am setting my mind,
things o'er which Christ is presiding;
Not on the temporals of earth below,
where the mundane things are passing.

Since on the cross of Christ I died that Day,
with Christ in God I am hidden;
The earthly part of me I mortify,
by the Spirit's strength now given.

My new self is being renewed daily,
in a knowledge that is true and richer;
As the Spirit impresses God's image—
in my mind things become clearer.

The peace of Christ guides my every decision,
and gratitude fills my days;
Christ's own words have found a home in my heart,
all my life is lived to his praise.

The Speaking Word

Colossians 3:1-3; 10, 15, NLT

Since I have been raised up with Christ my Lord,
Since you have been raised to new life with Christ . . .

On things above I am setting my mind,
. . . set your sights on the realities of heaven, where Christ sits in the place of honor at God's right hand. Think about the things of heaven, not the things of earth.

Since on the cross of Christ I died that Day,
For you died to this life, and your real life is hidden with Christ in God.

My new self is being renewed daily,
. . . and be renewed as you learn to know your Creator and become like him.

The peace of Christ guides my every decision,
And let the peace that comes from Christ rule in your hearts. For as members of one body you are called to live in peace.

Oaks of Righteousness

They will be called oaks of righteousness,
a planting of the LORD for the display of his splendor.
— Isaiah 61:3, NIV

In the midst of moral confusion,
Surrounded by darkness and despair,
God has planted his servants,
Who breathe in Heaven's air.

With roots reaching deeply into God:
His holiness, mercy, truth and love;
Each moment they are nourished
On nutrients from above.

Having weathered many storms and droughts,
More than once appearing far weaker;
What would have killed lesser souls,
Only makes these much stronger.

With their arms ever-stretching upward,
And faces gazing into the light;
They taste the dews each morning,
Drinking in the Spirit's might.

While many others lie on the ground,
Casualties to the flesh and shame;
These stalwarts have stood the test of time,
Protected through Jesus' name.

They are the Lord's own chosen planting,
Displaying his splendor all around;
"Oaks of righteousness," he says.
May their number, Lord, abound.

The Day of Christ

. . . so that in the day of Christ I may glory
that I did not run in vain or labor in vain.
— Philippians 2:16

In his classic volume *Purity of Heart is to Will One Thing*, Danish theologian Søren Kierkegaard (1813-1855) offers this sobering insight regarding the Day of Christ: "In eternity you as an individual will only be asked about your faith and your faithfulness. There will be absolutely no asking about whether you were entrusted with much or little, whether you were given many talents of silver to work with or whether you were given a hundred-pound weight to carry. But you will be asked only about your faith and your faithfulness."[24]

Sobering words, indeed!

In recently reading the inspired writings of the Apostle Paul, I have been impressed again that he was possessed with an overriding desire that his converts remain true in this world until the Day of Christ. But interestingly enough, he not only wanted his converts to be faithful and persevere to the end so that they themselves would be able to give a good accounting at the Day of Christ, but he also wanted them to remain faithful so that it would be revealed at the Day of Christ that his own labors among them would not prove to have been worthless.

Faithfulness for the Philippians—and for all Christians—

involved, on the positive side, obedience: "Therefore, my beloved, as you have always obeyed . . ." (2:12); on the negative side: the absence of grumbling and questioning: "Do all things without grumbling or questioning . . ." (2:14). Why does Paul hope for such behavior? "that you may be blameless and innocent, children of God without blemish in the midst of a crooked and twisted generation, among whom you shine as lights in the world, holding fast to the word of life . . ." (2:15-16).

Then Paul reveals more. He is not only concerned that these believers will remain faithful to Christ in order that they will be seen as shining lights in this world, he is also concerned as to how his own ministry among the Philippians will be viewed at the Day of Christ: "so that in the day of Christ I may glory that I did not run in vain or labor in vain." (2:16). The Christlike lives of Paul's converts, would be shown at the Day of Christ that his ministry in Philippi had not been wasted, worthless, and in vain.

How much ministry is in vain, worthless?

According to Paul, if our efforts fail to produce changed lives—shining lights in this world—all the time, energy, and funds we have expended will be for naught on the Day of Christ.

A Parable of Trees

Of all the trees in the forest,
One stood above as the tallest:
Majestic in height,
A beautiful sight.
Exulting in its high stature,
It peered down on all trees lesser.

Another tree was rarely seen,
Never thinking to ever preen:
Diminutive size,
Not winning a prize.
Lower than all others standing,
Contented without comparing.

There was a green tree flourishing,
Rich in fruit, it was nourishing:
Symmetric in shape,
Its branches did drape.
Greener was it than all its peers,
Not seeming to have any fears.

Of all the trees, one was driest;
The soil was poor, the rain lightest:
With withering roots,
It could bear no fruits.
This tree's future was dismal most,
Hope for survival all but lost.

"But that all may know who I am,
For every tree I have a plan:
The high to bring down,
The low to crown,
The greenest of all uprooting,
The dry tree bring to flourishing.
I am the LORD; I have spoken,
This plan to perform unbroken."

The High and the Low

"All the trees of the field will know that I am the LORD;
I bring down the high tree, exalt the low tree, dry up the green tree
and make the dry tree to flourish. I am the LORD;
I have spoken, and I will perform it."
— Ezekiel 17:24, NASB

Fallen man is preoccupied with where he perceives himself to be on "Life's Ladder of Success." Regardless of one's economic status, social standing, occupation, educational attainments, or giftedness, prideful man intuitively compares himself to those *above* and *below.*

Living in Babylon among his exiled people some 2600 years ago, Ezekiel, the prophet-priest, was God's messenger to proud kings and people. Because Judah's arrogant king had stubbornly refused to listen to the prophets, God would bring him "low." In his place another would be elevated—given a "high" place—effectively fulfilling God's ultimate purposes for his people.

It's tough being a "high tree" and remain humble. With his usual insight, C. S. Lewis (1898-1963) offers this comment on the subject of pride: "A proud man is always looking down on things and people: and, of course, as long as you are looking down, you cannot see something above you"[25] (see Mt. 5:8). Lewis notes that the "something above" is in reality God. We cannot see God as long as we think of ourselves as a "high tree." To *see* God is to be pure in heart.

One should not be surprised to see the *world* full of "high trees." We expect that. But to its shame, the contemporary church has rolled out the carpet to the "high trees." We feverishly parade our successes and flaunt our statistics. With blaring trumpets and rolling drums, we heap honors upon one another while turning a deaf ear to the honor of God. We love being tall trees! We're in love with ourselves.

When does spiritual renewal (revival) begin? When the "high" tree bows low . . . before God . . . and then before men. How does revival continue in the heart and life of the believer? By living as a "low tree." "God opposes the proud, but gives grace to the humble" (James 4:6). Of course, a truly "low tree" never thinks of himself as a "low tree." He knows more than any other that apart from the heavenly Arborist he is full of filthy hubris. In his time, God promises to exalt the "low trees."

Prayer: *O God, my Father, show me the pride of my heart; and what your eyes see, may I own and confess, bringing all the putrid mess to the cross of Christ. Amen.*

Lord, Make Me a Pillar

"The one who conquers, I will make him a pillar in the temple of my God. Never shall he go out of it, and I will write on him the name of my God."
— Revelation 3:12

Lord, make me a pillar in your sanctuary,
one who has been made strong by your Spirit.
I want a will and love that will never vary—
to seek your righteousness . . . and to live it.

I am surrounded by compromise and weakness;
the love of many daily grows cold.
Will I join with them in their moral sickness,
or abide in Christ and in him live bold?

"If you want in my temple to be a pillar,
to have a love and will that is made strong,
You must by my Spirit be an overcomer,
rejecting every form of sin and wrong.

To each one who follows me with humility,
overcoming the flesh, the world, and sin,
I will inscribe God's name on him indelibly,
making him a pillar of strength within."

Whatever the cost, O Lord, make me a pillar;
strengthen me mightily without, within.
By your Spirit I shall be an overcomer—
then, please, write your name on me with your pen.

Weakness & Strength

So to keep me from becoming conceited because of the surpassing greatness of the revelations, a thorn was given me in the flesh, a messenger of Satan to harass me, to keep me from becoming conceited.
— 2 Corinthians 12:7, NIV

One of those paradoxical principles of the Kingdom of God is that we are only made strong by first becoming weak—and staying weak.

Unsanctified humanity seeks to be strong—a strong politician, a strong parent, a strong professor, a strong pastor, a strong leader, a strong person, a strong Christian. In our desire and need to be strong, we manipulate people in order to advance our objectives and achieve our goals. Our arrogant impatience with people and Providence are obstacles to overcome while we get on with our more important agenda for success. Our fallen and diseased egos are intolerant of those we view as rivals, and dismissive of those we perceive as inferior to us. A well-enthroned *self* rules and doesn't easily bow—to God or men.

Whether such an individual is in the church or outside, matters little. Inside his heart he is the same. Whether he considers himself to be an evangelical Christian or a Protestant liberal is immaterial. He is ultimately in charge. A self-ruled, man-managed, autonomous, sinful ego is at the helm. Such a person pays only lip service to the lordship of Jesus Christ and acts as though he has never heard of the Holy Spirit.

Recently I received in the mail a multi-page, full-color, slick advertisement from a church growth organization. It was promoting how one's church was assured of growth if their plan was carefully followed. I scanned the 8-10 page layout to see if there was even one reference to the Holy Spirit—after all, the book of Acts is a history of the church's growth in the first century, and the Holy Spirit was the fundamental Agent responsible for that growth. There was not even a cursory reference to the Trinity's third Person. All that *glitters* is not of God!

The Holy Spirit can only work effectively through the weak—those who have become weak enough to die to self-rule, self-interest, self-promotion, self-sovereignty. Such a person was Jacob of old. Facing a real and present crisis, this Old Testament patriarch went down by a brook to pray, to wrestle. Jacob was strong—too strong for God to use mightily. He must become weak; he must acknowledge his sinfulness, his vulnerabilities, his failures. He must confess who he was essentially—a deceiver.

Jacob wanted to be blessed (Did he pray the Jabez' prayer?); God knew he needed first to be *bruised.* How we Christians want to be blessed—to be strong.

Only those weakened by God are strong. This is God's way. Shall we go down to the brook?

The Vinedresser's Knife

As a branch in your vineyard,
Lord, I want to be fruitful;
To produce a rich harvest
for you—I would be grateful.

"Child, to be a fruitful branch
in this season of your life,
Let me cut away from you
all that's useless with my knife."

Lord, is there no other way
I can produce fruit for you;
Some way that's far less painful
than pruning that which I grew?

"The only way is my way,
as painful as it may be;
By submitting to my knife,
you'll bear fruit abundantly."

Then, Lord, gently take your knife—
I trustingly surrender;
For to bear rich Spirit-fruit,
magnifies my Vinedresser.

Pruned to Produce

*". . . and every branch that bears fruit,
He prunes it so that it may bear more fruit."*
—John 15:2b, NASB

Anyone would have to be a sadomasochist to enjoy being cut on. I have only undergone a surgeon's knife once in my adult life, and then, of course, I had the benefits of modern day anesthesia. I didn't *feel* a thing.

It has been quite the contrast in my walk with Christ these past fifty years. Often my Vinedresser has taken up his *knife* and deftly removed that which would hinder growth and fruitfulness. Unlike physical surgery accompanied by anesthesia, I have *felt* my heavenly Vinedresser's incisions—sometimes through tears.

I am told that before pruning, an average grapevine may have 200-300 buds, all of which are capable of producing fruit. However, if left unpruned, the number of grape clusters would be excessive; the vine would be incapable of producing a large crop or sustaining adequate vegetative growth.

The reason the vinedresser prunes his vine regularly is to obtain maximum yields of high quality grapes and to allow adequate vegetative growth for the following season. Therefore pruning is essential.

Pruning takes both knowledge and wisdom. It must be done by skilled experts and at the proper time of year. And the vinedresser must be thoroughly acquainted with his vines in order to prune his plants with balance. One university horticulture department says: "The degree or extent of pruning is dictated by vine vigor. Vine vigor is determined by estimating the amount of the previous season's growth. This concept is called 'balanced pruning.'"[26] The expert vinedresser knows what to cut away, what to leave, and when to cut.

So it is with the Christian's Vinedresser. Desiring that we may produce luscious fruit to his praise and glory, he wants to excise from our life everything that will hinder us from being a fruitful branch. And he can be trusted to remove from our heart and lives only what is necessary in order to achieve maximum growth.

Only by willingly and lovingly surrendering to our Vinedresser's knife, can we be cleansed from the fleshly excesses that stunt our spiritual growth. While the process may be painful at times, we must always remember that he who was "wounded for our transgressions" will never use his *knife* on us without a sovereign purpose.

The healthiest branches bring the greatest joy to their Vinedresser.

A Channel of Blessing

Make me, O Lord, one of your channels of blessing,
a life poured out in service to you.
Filled with Jesus' love and compassion for others,
may Christ be seen in all that I do.

In the presence of selfish ambition and strife,
a bearer of holy peace make me.
Save me from all pettiness that drives men apart,
promoting the Spirit's unity.

Where cruel pride pervades men's thoughtless agenda,
using others to achieve their end;
Show me the footprints of him who became a slave,
stooping low to serve—willing to bend.

In this impersonal world of sorrow and stress,
where many callously look away;
May I bring Christ's presence to your hurting children—
comfort and cheer, just like the sun's ray.

When an obstruction emerges in this channel,
let me not sin attempt to excuse;
But flee directly to the cross of Christ Jesus—
grace to receive that I you might use.

Make me, O Lord, one of your channels of blessing,
a life poured out in service to you.
I seek no gain or rewards down here;
I'm content to keep your smile in view.

Seven Channels

This is the word of the LORD to Zerubbabel: "You will never be able to fulfill my mission, while depending on your own abilities and resources or putting your trust in the influence and abilities of other people. Look to me alone—the adequate source of all you need."
— Zechariah 4:6, RIT

Our Father in Heaven yearningly desires that each of his children be a channel of grace and blessing in this dark, fallen world. Is his desire your desire?

The only way God's desire can be effectively approximated in each of our lives is that we make a conscious and total surrender of our lives to his Son, the Lord Jesus Christ, and then walk day by day keeping in step with the blessed Holy Spirit.

If we desire to be a conduit of mercy and grace but fail to walk in obedience and fellowship with our Lord, then our desire is tainted with a sinful pride and self-centered ego—it is a desire to be great in our eyes and in the eyes of others. If we do accomplish anything—even in the church—while it may result in the applause of men, it is incapable of bringing true glory and honor to Christ. We cannot promote ourselves and Christ at the same time.

As he surveyed the awesome assignment to rebuild the house of worship, Zerubbabel felt completely inadequate. Knowing he felt such inadequacy, a vision of God's sufficiency was given to the prophet-priest Zechariah to share with Zerubbabel. It was a vision of two olive trees furnishing an abundant supply of oil to a menorah—a lampstand with seven channels.

Just like many in the church today, the prophet didn't understand the meaning of the vision. Thus, the Lord gave the interpretation:

This is the word of the LORD to Zerubbabel: "You will never be able to fulfill my mission, while depending on your own abilities and resources or putting your trust in the influence and abilities of other people. Look to me alone—the adequate source of all you need" (Zech. 4:6, RIT).

Do you wish to be a channel of blessing, dear reader? Then invite the blessed Holy Spirit to cleanse your polluted, ego-ridden channel, allowing the *oil* to flow freely—the oil of the Holy Spirit. You will thus be God's light and channel of blessing wherever he places you.

I am Lost

I am lost—
and you formed a committee
to discuss my lostness.

I am lost—
and you wrote a manual
about how to find me.

I am lost—
and you were content
to only pray for me.

I am lost—
and you meet every week
to study about my absence.

I am lost—
and you appointed only one person
to search for me.

I am lost—
and you travel miles to listen to an expert
talk about people like me.

I am lost—
and you say
I could be lost forever.

I am lost—
and you built a special building
for me to find.

I am lost—
and you sent thousands of dollars
to someone else to find me.

I am lost—
in your neighborhood,
in your office—
when will you start looking for me?

A Friend to the Lost

"For the Son of Man came to seek and to save the lost."
— Luke 19:10

Zacchaeus was lost and didn't know it, not unlike most lost people in every age. It usually takes some time before a person discovers that he or she is lost That's true geographically speaking, as well as spiritually.

I can remember the day as though it just happened. When just in our teens, my friend Dennis and I were taking a hike through a dense forest. It was a beautiful summer day in the Brown County woods. We laughed, ran, investigated—just like any two boys would do. We were enjoying the forest and our time together. But then it happened—we suddenly realized we didn't know where we were or how to get back to his aunt's house. We were lost! And then we became fearful, for the sun was about to set.

I'm sure neither Dennis nor I—before or since—have ever talked to a dog as much as we did in the evening twilight that day. It so happened that his aunt's dog, Yellow, went with us on that eventful hike. After learning of our plight, we started talking to Yellow in animated tones: "Yellow, show us the way home! Show us the way back! Come on, Yellow, show us! Show us!" And Yellow never failed those two scared kids. He led us back home.

The Lord Jesus Christ was—and still is—a compassionate friend to *lost* people. Zacchaeus was lost—lost from God. Oh, God knew where this wandering Jew was, but Zacchaeus didn't know where he himself was. Jesus went to find him. That's why he came—to seek and to save lost people. He came to lead people back to the Father, back to their true Home.

God has called you and me to actively seek out the lost and bring them to Jesus, bring them Home to their true resting place. Augustine of Hippo's (354-430) mother, Monica, followed her prodigal son for years—with her tears. After finally coming Home, Augustine wrote: "Thou has made us for Thyself, O God, and we are restless until we find our rest in Thee." The lost one had come Home.

Let us join with the Son of Man in being a real friend to lost people.

Prayer: *O Christ of God, forgive me for my indifference to lost people. Renew in me your passion for wandering souls. By your grace and mercy, empower me to be your instrument in showing some lonely soul the way Home. Amen.*

The Eyes of the Lord

O God, your eyes are constantly searching
for a heart perfect and true,
Searching for God-hungry men and women,
fully devoted to you.

Wishing to reveal your strength and power
in this present day and age,
You are looking for sanctified vessels
you can easily manage.

"Where is the Christian," you yearningly ask,
"Whose heart is completely mine;
Who relies only on me and not self,
dwelling always in the Vine?"

O God, I so want to be that person
who catches your roaming eyes;
One who has a heart where only you live
and your smile is his chief prize.

"Dear child, I'm delighted, as your Father
to hear such aspiration;
Let me now cleanse, fill, then mold and test you
for a strategic mission."

As God's eyes are searching for that person
whom he wishes to support,
Will the eyes of God rest on you and me?—
is the question of import.

The Wholehearted

"For the eyes of the LORD move to and fro throughout the earth that He may strongly support those whose heart is completely His."
— 2 Chronicles 16:9, NASB

King Asa died in the forty-first year of his reign. That is a long time to be king—even a longer time to be a *godly* king. And that was the problem. Asa failed to persevere in godliness.

Out of a total of some four decades on the throne, Asa served the Lord with a whole heart only twenty-five per cent of those years—ten years.

For ten years this king was a righteous reformer. He cleansed the land of its foreign altars and gods. He led the way in seeking the Lord and observing the law and commandments. He constructed fortified cities throughout Judah's territories. Asa was a builder, a leader. And he was very successful—successful as God counts success. For ten years he "did good and right in the eyes of the LORD his God" (2 Chron. 14:2).

It is only a rare person who can handle large success—large success given as a result of God's blessing—successfully. While millions of our contemporaries have prayed the prayer of Jabez—"Oh that you would bless me . . ." (1 Chron. 4:10)—I wonder how many of them realize that God can't trust them with his blessing—not yet.

At the pinnacle of Asa's success and blessing, he failed miserably. What had characterized his life and reign for ten years—total reliance upon God—he forfeited in a moment of fleshly weakness. He chose to rely on man—himself and others.

The renowned evangelist of the Hebrides Revival, Duncan Campbell (1898-1972), knew the heights of God's blessing as well as the depths of personal powerlessness. After being used mightily by God, he wrote years later, "For 17 years I moved in [a] barren wilderness." Why? Because he started enjoying the sound of being introduced as "Campbell of the Mid Argyll Revival." Fortunately he repented of his prideful heart and God once more was able to bless his ministry.[27]

By the sanctifying ministry of the blessed Holy Spirit, there is one thing each of us can render to the Lord—a heart which is "completely His."

Do you want to be used of God? Then ponder the words of the prophet to Asa: "For the eyes of the LORD move to and fro throughout the earth that He may strongly support those whose heart is completely His."

Prayer of Total Consecration

O God, my heavenly Father, through the gracious entreaties of your Son, the Lord Jesus Christ, as well as by the urgent appeals of your holy Apostles, you have called me to leave all, to give all, to love you with all my heart, soul, mind and strength.

> *"If anyone would come after me, let him deny himself and take up his cross daily and follow me" (Lk. 9:23).*
>
> *"And you shall love the Lord your God with all your heart and with all your soul and with all your mind and with all your strength" (Mk. 12:30).*
>
> *"I appeal to you therefore, brothers, by the mercies of God, to present your bodies as a living sacrifice, holy and acceptable to God, which is your spiritual worship" (Rom. 12:1-2).*

I hear the gentle, persistent voice of your Holy Spirit calling me to total surrender—a total surrender to the Lord Jesus Christ. My flesh shrinks from relinquishing total control. I have been accustomed too long of being in charge. My pride and sinful ego hesitate. My mind is torn. My sinful self fears abandonment to you, O God. And, yet, I hear the call, the still small voice of the Good Shepherd:

> *"Behold, I stand at the door and knock; if anyone hears My voice and opens the door, I will come in to him and will dine with him, and he with Me" (Rev. 3:20 NASB).*

I want so much to will your will without reservation and conflict. I do desire that Christ would be seated on the throne of my heart without a rival. I am hungering and thirsting after only your righteousness. I crave only you; my heart pants for the living God. O Father, in utter desperation I yield my total self to you. Yes, Lord; I say yes to the Spirit's call. I give myself to you—totally. I entrust the totality of my life to you. And have you not assured every honest seeker that whatever has been sincerely offered to you, you accept and sanctify to the praise of your Son, the Lord Jesus Christ?

> *"Whatever touches the altar shall become holy" (Exodus 29:37).*

With the deepest gratitude, O Christ, my Altar, I humbly thank you for accepting me, embracing me, cleansing me through your shed blood.

All for Jesus, all for Jesus!
All my being's ransomed powers:
All my thoughts and words and doings.
All my days and all my hours.

Let my hands perform His bidding.
Let my feet run in His ways;
Let my eyes see Jesus only.
Let my lips speak forth His praise.[28]

All praise to you, holy Father, for hearing the prayer of one of your unworthy, thirsty servants. In the strong name of Christ, your Son. Amen.

Canaan

If I could take you to a land
where the milk and honey flows;
If I could show you Eschol's grapes
that only my Vinedresser grows—
Would you come?

This place is not without mountains;
its valleys are more than a few.
But the rivers here are many,
in the morning there's always dew.
Would you come?

The burdens here are much lighter;
peace is ev'rywhere to be found.
Joy fills all the fertile valleys;
God's love and holiness abound.
Will you come?

You say, "That is the very place
my spirit has been longing for,
Since God brought me out of Egypt
many wilderness years before!
I want to come."

But first you must cross the Jordan,
leaving all self-interest behind.
You must die to self and others,
ev'rything on the altar bind.
Will you still come?

"By God's grace I do die to self,
looking to Jesus, not others.
I bind my all on God's altar
and now see the parting waters.
I come!"

A Promised Rest

So then, there remains a Sabbath rest for the people of God . . .
— Hebrews 4:9

The writer of the Hebrews' letter clearly saw Canaan as a destination to be entered and enjoyed in this present life by Old Testament Israel. It was a land rich in natural resources, described eight times in the Old Testament as a "land flowing with milk and honey."

Canaan was God's promised gift to a people who had been delivered from Egyptian slavery. It was a gift Yahweh intended his covenant family to enter within a few weeks following their miraculous Red Sea crossing. However, because of unbelief and disobedience, Israel turned away from her promised inheritance and wandered aimlessly for forty years in the Arabian peninsula. Those years were characterized by defeat, disappointment, disillusionment, and frequently despair. And yet, God was gracious to his chosen people and mercifully provided them with water and food, as well as delivering them on occasion from destructive forces. Finally, however, under Joshua's leadership, Israel entered Canaan and little by little drove out its entrenched enemies.

Speaking through the author of Hebrews, God views Canaan—the land he promised to Israel—as a prototype of the inheritance he wishes to give his people in every age. This inheritance is available in *this* life, not some distant eschatological future, following death.

This Canaan land inheritance is called a "rest" in Hebrews 4. And it is a rest God wishes all of his people to experience and enjoy in *this* life. "Therefore, while the promise of entering his rest still stands, let us fear lest any of you should seem to have failed to reach it" (Heb. 4:1). Remember, these words were addressed to Christians, but Christians who had not yet entered into this promised rest.

Israel, under Joshua's leadership, never experienced the existential fullness of this promised rest. The *rest* under Joshua was essentially material and physical. The rest spoken of in Hebrews 4 is spiritual, a Sabbath rest, an inner rest. "For if Joshua had given them rest, God would not have spoken of another day later on. So then, there remains a Sabbath rest for the people of God, for whoever has entered God's rest has also rested from his works as God did from his" (Heb. 4:8-10).

This reminds me of a dear minister friend who has recently experienced a deep personal renewal. He says for years he had been living the Christian life and ministering in his own strength. Now he has "rested from his works" and entered God's rest.

What about you, my friend, are you enjoying the fruits of Canaan? Have you entered this Sabbath rest, a rest from all your own works?

O Spirit of God

O Spirit of God,
my boat lies so still
in the waters of vast need.
Send your holy breeze
as I set my sail
to follow a new course
marked out for me.

O Spirit of God,
the embers burn low
on the altar made for you.
Blow repeatedly
as I yield my will
until a brighter flame
your eyes shall see.

O Spirit of God,
my love is so dry;
you deserve far more from me.
As I hold real still,
pour in me your oil,
then I'll rise refreshed
to do your will.

O Spirit of God,
the clay is too strong
as your hands try to mold me.
Press deep in my soul,
until my self bends
to your perfect design
and kind control.

Wind of God

And suddenly there came from heaven a sound like a mighty rushing wind, and it filled the entire house where they were sitting.
— Acts 2:2

It was a crisp October morning as I sat in the car overlooking beautiful Montagu Bay. My vehicle had been provided to my wife Emily and me by our gracious hosts, Sir Durward (he was the first Olympic gold medal winner from the Bahamas) and Lady Holly Knowles, during my week of ministry among the dear people at the Nassau Ebenezer Methodist Church.

As I viewed the wide assortment of commercial and pleasure boats on the bay that day, I was struck by the sight of the sailboats being pushed gently along by the wind. Tilting slightly to the side, these motorless vessels—each majestic in its own right—made no sound, except that caused by nature, as they effortlessly pursued their destinations.

The power propelling these sailboats was unseen and unheard, but the effects were real and observable. Vessels, which apart from the wind would remain motionless and useless, were traveling according to plan. They were fulfilling the very purpose of their respective creators.

Of the several symbols for the Spirit of God in the Scriptures, wind is one. Interestingly enough, both the Hebrew and

Greek words for "Spirit" are also two of the same words rendered as "wind." Wind is a mysterious force, providing energy and power, motion and refreshment, evoking awe among its respectful witnesses. So is the Spirit of God.

Just as the mysterious, sovereign Spirit generates life in men and women dead in their sins (see John 3), so this same Spirit empowers Christ's thirsty-hearted disciples with an energy to do the will of the Father in this life: "And suddenly there came from heaven a sound like a mighty rushing wind. . . . And they were all filled with the Holy Spirit" (Acts 2:2-3); "be filled with the Spirit" (Eph. 5:18).

It is one of God's axioms: Whoever by God's grace, will hoist their *sail* to catch the *Wind*, the Spirit of God will fill that person, achieving his purpose in such a life to the glory and praise of the Lord Jesus Christ.

Count on it—to lift that sail will *cost* you something. But not to lift it will prove immeasurably more costly to you and Christ's church.

Without the Wind of God our *boats* are useless. Pay the price. Unfurl your sail and stand in awe as you watch the Spirit of God take you where you've never been, use you as you have never been used, and shape you as you've never been shaped.

Going Deeper

You say you want to go deeper
than you have ever gone before,
To plumb the depths of God vaster—
his love and holiness explore?

You long to be more like Jesus,
reflecting daily his image—
Aspiring to his own likeness,
emulating our Lord's visage?

Your desire is to be fruitful,
bringing joy to your Father's heart?
Like Christ, you want to be faithful,
serving others, doing your part?

Then, for now, be very still.

Is your will to let God crush you,
to bruise where your ego's entrenched,
To die to the I *inside you,*
to repent of his Spirit quenched?

If so, walk up Calvary's hill,
leaving sin and selfism behind.
There, let God in you something kill,
till he can form in you Christ's mind.

You must never leave that hill.

True Greatness

"But whoever would be great among you must be your servant, and whoever would be first among you must be slave of all."
— Mark 10:43-44.

As fledgling followers of the Lord Jesus, the chosen Twelve did not understand what true greatness was all about. Greatness to them was about position, prestige, titles, being first, and authority. They still loved the praise of men more than the praise of God. To serve others was to be done . . . as long as they were seen and got credit for it. Silent service, unnoticed service, lowly service—these were not even on their "radar screens."

When James and John on one occasion expressed their desire to be given prominent positions in Christ's future kingdom reign, they vented their natural desires: they wanted to "rule," they wanted to be "great," they wanted to be "first."

It was a teaching moment. Jesus replied that leadership in his kingdom was just the opposite of worldly leadership: "But whoever would be great among you must be your servant, and whoever would be first among you must be slave of all" (Mk. 10:43-44).

Through the ages, the church and her leaders have often forgotten Christ's teaching about what makes for true greatness. True greatness in the church is not synonymous with titles of office, position, and academic degrees. True greatness is not to be confused with pulpit oratory, well-trained voices, or wealth. True greatness is not about miracles, signs and wonders, and busy-ness in the kingdom of God.

True greatness, as Christ views it, is an attitude—a servant attitude. A true servant doesn't serve for what praise he or she will receive from men. Christian servants perform their loving acts of service, striving for faithfulness and excellence. They serve with an eye to please their Master in Heaven. They don't seek to do great things; they seek to do small things in a great way. They seek to do their duty.

One of the most meaningful poems George MacDonald (1824-1905) ever wrote was written to one of his young sons by the name of Willie. Willie evidently aspired to do something *great*. Knowing of his son's misplaced aspirations, the wise father wrote a sixty-three stanza poem to remind the boy what true greatness is all about. One stanza reads:

The man who was Lord of fate,
Born in an ox's stall,
Was great because he was much too great
To care about greatness at all.[29]

Not I, but Christ

I have been crucified with Christ,
nailed to the Cross was I—

the I twisted inward,
the I blinded outward,

the I driven to succeed,
the I grasping with greed,

the I never in wrong,
the I with no true song,

the I self-directed,
the I self-affected.

I have been crucified with Christ,
nevertheless I live—

not the old I resides,
for Christ in me abides.

I have been crucified with Christ,
and the life I now live I . . .

live by faith in the Son,
by whose love I've been won,

who defeated the I
when he gave his last cry.

Ego

I have been crucified with Christ.
— Galatians 2:20

I once heard a church board member say that the actions and reactions he witnessed among his fellow Christians were little different than those he saw on a daily basis among his fellow corporate executives. Why is it that Christians sometimes behave no differently than the common sinner?

A renowned evangelist said years ago, "While the sins of the *flesh* have slain its thousands, the sins of the *spirit* have slain its tens-of-thousands." Of course, the evangelist wasn't using the term "flesh" in Paul's ethical usage of the word. Strictly speaking, the flesh encompasses sins of the "spirit" (unchristlike attitudes) as well as every other action contrary to a life lived in the Spirit.

What is the answer to unchristlike attitudes and actions among Christians? Paul provides the solution in his own personal testimony in Galatians 2:20: "I have been crucified with Christ. It is no longer I who live, but Christ who lives in me. And the life I now live in the flesh I live by faith in the Son of God, who loved me and gave himself for me."

Crucifixion is both objective and subjective—something done *for* us and something done *in* us. Christ took Paul with him to the cross. Christ not only died *for* Paul, Paul died *with*

Christ. But Paul had to appropriate that redemptive fact through faith—which he did. But there's more. Paul said "It is no longer I (Greek: *ego*) who live." Here's one of the essential keys to successful Christian living: something fundamentally and radically happened to Paul's *ego* when he affirmed his death with Christ on the cross—his ego was forever altered, his unsanctified/uncrucified ego no longer dominated his life. But we can't live the Christian life successfully merely with a crucified ego. Paul says his ego not only died with Christ, but that Christ himself moved in and became a dynamic presence: "Christ lives in me."

Such a life was transformative and radically different in contrast to the life Paul previously lived: "And the life I now live ..."—right now—in the very present. Paul says in effect: "I no longer exult in my self-righteousness. I am no longer governed by a sinful, fallen, driven, self-centered ego. My carnal pride and religious reputation have been nailed to the cross—no, more accurately—*I* (my *ego*) have been nailed to Christ's cross and I remain there to this very day."

A crucified person, indwelt by the living Christ, is the church's greatest force and the world's greatest need.

Prayer: *O God, I give my consent; drive your nails deep into my ego until Christ, and Christ alone, reigns within.*

O Lord, Renew Me

My eyes are dry,
my heart is numb;
The world is lost,
my voice is mum—
O Lord, renew me!

Temptation's near,
Heaven is dim;
The fire burns low,
my love is slim—
O Lord, renew me!

My prayers are weak,
faith is feeble;
My strength is gone,
the will's in trouble—
O Lord, renew me!

The world's around,
the flesh is close;
My heart is cold,
the gold turned dross—
O Lord, renew me!

I bow down low,
I look up high;
Confess my need,
begin to sigh—
O Lord, renew me!

I feel his Wind,
I set my sails;
The will's made strong,
his love prevails—
O Lord, you have renewed me!

Day-by-Day Renewal

Though our outer self is wasting away,
our inner self is being renewed day by day.
— 2 Corinthians 4:16

As I write this, the North American continent is undergoing its perennial renewal. Springtime has arrived once again. Trees and fields are awaking from their season of dormancy and sleep. Renewed life is everywhere present.

In nature the seasons are cyclical, with months intervening between spring and the following winter. In one's walk in the Spirit, *daily* spiritual renewal is every Christian's privilege, and should be every believer's desired daily goal.

Day-by-day renewal is made possible by the Spirit's presence in the life of every regenerated Christian, but it is often a neglected privilege. How Christ longs to be refreshingly near to every follower. And yet we regularly allow the mundane and trivial to crowd out what is primary and essential.

For forty years in their wilderness wanderings, the old covenant people of God were daily sustained by bread from Heaven each morning and given meat every evening. In order for their daily physical needs to be met, God instructed them to gather the manna before the dew dried. For those who rose too late, to their loss, they discovered no food. The provisions for physical renewal had been forfeited.

To experience daily renewal means more than to *survive*. To be renewed by the Spirit day-by-day is to *thrive*.

Was not daily spiritual renewal the key to the apostle Paul's abounding joy and passionate love for the Lord Jesus Christ? How could he claim that he was constantly "afflicted in every way, but not crushed; perplexed, but not driven to despair; persecuted, but not forsaken; struck down, but not destroyed"? How? Because he also testified, "Though our outer self is wasting away, our inner self is being renewed day by day" (see 2 Cor. 4:7-18).

While identifying himself just as human as any other Christian ("we have this treasure in *jars of clay*"), yet Paul knew if this "treasure" was to always be dynamically effective in his life, he must be renewed daily so that he could see the face of Jesus clearly, as revealed by Word and Spirit.

How we suffer because of the failure to allow the Spirit to renew our daily strength. Instead of rising up with wings like eagles, we run and are *weary*; we walk and are *faint*.

Daily manna awaits us. Let us gather our portion for the glory of God and our soul's health. Only then are we equipped to serve . . . and to conquer.

Renewal

My prayers are so listless,
My love is so cold;
My heart feels so empty,
My vision on hold.

My tears flow too slowly,
My stomach too full;
My hands droop so heavy,
My soul lacks your pull.

Forgive, O Lord, I pray,
Failures to be strong;
Make my heart like yours—
Free from ev'ry wrong.

O Christ of Calvary,
Fan anew your flame;
Burn brightly within me—
Claim all in your name.

Spirit of Pentecost,
Send in me your wind;
Fill every yielded part—
Strengthen as I bend.

Pour your oil within me,
Inner man renew.
Your fragrant presence bring,
Till Christ's in full view.

One God-Reliant Life

Indeed, we felt that we had received the sentence of death.
But that was to make us rely not on ourselves
but on God who raises the dead.
— 2 Corinthians 1:9

One characteristic marking the life and ministry of the Apostle Paul is this: he lived a God-reliant life.

Ever after his life-transforming encounter with the living Christ on his way to Damascus that one eventful day, Paul lived under the guidance of God. Once his life had been flesh-directed: making choices generated from his sinful, fallen nature and will. But following his revelation of Christ and filling of the Spirit, the former fire-breathing persecutor of Christians becomes the humble, obedient follower of the Lord Jesus Christ. Once a slave to the sinful passions of the flesh, receiving a new heart he became a willing slave of the One who himself took on the form of a slave to offer himself as an atoning sacrifice for the sins of all mankind.

Whether it is the book of Acts—which records many of Paul's works of ministry—or his 13 epistles, one will search in vain to find a hint in this apostle's life of anything but a life of total submission and reliance on God.

For an example of his leading a God-reliant life, take this one section from Paul's letter to the Corinthian Church (2 Cor. 1). At the close of his exhortation on suffering, comfort and affliction (vv. 3-8), he writes: "For we do not want you to be ignorant, brothers, of the affliction we experienced in Asia. For we were so utterly burdened beyond our strength that we despaired of life itself. Indeed, we felt that we had received the sentence of death. *But that was to make us rely not on ourselves but on God who raises the dead"* (1:8-9, emphasis added). Here Paul reveals his sensitivity to the providences of God in his life, reminding him of his need for continual reliance upon God.

In the same chapter, while defending his reason for changing his mind as to when he would revisit the church, he asks a probing rhetorical question: "Do I make my plans according to the flesh ...?" The obvious answer is, no, he does not.

I'm reminded of the surprise of E. Stanley Jones (1884-1973)—Methodist missionary for over 50 years to India—upon learning after he was appointed by the board that he would receive a salary (albeit, a very small one) as a missionary. This God-reliant man had accepted God's call to labor in a foreign land with no thought of any financial remuneration.

God doesn't call us to be foolish—though his callings may appear to be foolish to the natural eye. But he has called each of us to live a life of total reliance upon him, trusting him to make the critical choices for us.

Paying the Price

Do I want to finish strong,
and to the end run this race?
Shall I strive to reach the goal,
determined to keep the pace?

Lord, help me the price to pay
like men and women of old,
Who sought you with all their heart
and in faith were very bold.

Grant me grace to take action,
to lay aside every weight,
That which proves a distraction
and all that hinders my gait.

The sidelines are strewn with
undisciplined, careless men,
Who chose the convenient path,
failing to conquer within.

With a will made strong by yours,
to the side these weights I lay;
Easily entangled sin,
I wrench from my life today.

Now my eyes are fixed on Jesus,
having done with lesser things;
I run with ease of motion,
as it were on eagles' wings.

The Speaking Word

Do I want to finish strong . . .

I have fought the good fight, I have finished the race, I have kept the faith.

— 2 Timothy 4:8

Lord, help me the price to pay . . .

[7]Remember your leaders, those who spoke to you the word of God. Consider the outcome of their way of life, and imitate their faith. [8]Jesus Christ is the same yesterday and today and forever.

— Hebrews 13:7-8

Grant me grace to take action . . .

. . . let us strip off every weight that slows us down, especially the sin that so easily trips us up. And let us run with endurance the race God has set before us.

— Hebrews 12:1, NLT

The sidelines are strewn with . . .

But I discipline my body and keep it under control, lest after preaching to others I myself should be disqualified.

— 1 Corinthians 9:27

With a will made strong by yours . . .

. . . that according to the riches of his glory he may grant you to be strengthened with power through his Spirit in your inner being . . .

— Ephesians 3:16

Now my eyes are fixed on Jesus . . .

. . . keeping our eyes on Jesus . . .

— Hebrews 12:2

Faith in the Face of Failure

Expecting to see trees with blossoms laden,
I walked to my own orchard looking for gain;
But though with each tree great care had been taken,
it was plain to see that my efforts were vain.

Heartbroken, I turned and through my vineyard walked,
in hope of finding for my labor, success.
After carefully all the vines had been searched—
there was clearly no fruit but cause for distress.

Knowing that the fields were ready for harvest,
anxiously I went to take in the sight;
What I had hoped this year might be the largest—
was covered, row after row, with deadly blight.

Then to the lush fields I went in search of the flock;
there I found death instead of healthy, strong sheep.
Returning to the barn to check the livestock—
empty stalls I beheld and began to weep.

Falling to my knees in the barn that dark day,
filled with all kinds of pain and consternation;
I knew I had done my best in every way,
yet I was left with total devastation.

While there on my knees, that black day before God,
I somehow rejoiced in his great salvation;
And was able to look up—which might seem odd—
surrounded as I was with this destruction.

As I faced these failures, he helped me to pray,
"The Sovereign Lord is my strength, the Sovereign Lord!"
Quite suddenly all my dark fears fled away;
standing, I placed both feet firmly on his Word.

Though rugged the climb and I suffer greatly,
surefooted as a deer the Lord makes me be;
Bringing me over all mountains safely,
he proves his grace is all-sufficient for me.

(Based on Habakkuk 3:17-19.)

Habakkuk's Faith

Though the fig tree should not blossom . . . yet I will rejoice in the LORD; I will take joy in the God of my salvation.
— Habakkuk 3:17-18

An uninformed person might draw the conclusion, that a person who is filled and walking in the Spirit's power will always see the kind of Kingdom successes that he or she so earnestly desires. Such is most certainly not always the case.

Some of our Lord's most godly followers never saw—and never see—in this world, large numerical results from their faithful, Spirit-filled labors and ministries. Whether as a pastor, evangelist, Sunday school teacher, elder or deacon, or one who simply attends the means of grace faithfully—having no leadership role in the local church—God has on record an innumerable company of choice saints who love the Lord God with all their heart, soul, mind, and strength—and yet from man's vantage point their fruit is little.

It is true to the Word of God to say that God desires for his people to bear much fruit; this was the burden and vision that Jesus shared with his disciples in John 15. However, we must remember that God does not use man's *yardstick* in measuring spiritual results.

Habakkuk was a prophet who, from all appearances, saw little results from his ministry. And the fact is, most of the prophets never built mega-followings. But Habakkuk was God's man and God's mouthpiece to his generation. And his faith was so rock-solid in the God he served, that he knew God's grace would be sufficient for him even though Judah would eventually be plundered and laid waste by the Babylonians. This didn't take place until after the prophet's death, but when he offered his prayer (Hab. 3:17-19), he had no idea what God's prophetic timetable was.

By the strength of the Spirit, Habakkuk was given a resolute faith and was prepared to face the *whatever*. It is one thing to exercise faith in God when the harvest is large and the stalls filled to capacity, but what about when the opposite is the case? Living seven centuries before Christ, this Old Testament prophet lived what he taught: "The righteous will live by his faith" (2:4).

What about you and me, my friend? Will we walk with a steadfast faith in God, even when we are not *seeing* large returns for our labors?

By the grace of God, let us fall in line behind Habakkuk and exercise a faith in the faithful God . . . regardless.

A Fresh Vision of Jesus

I need a fresh vision of Jesus—
the One who turned the water into wine;
the One who took what was fully offered
and filled the thirsty from the Vine.

I need a fresh vision of Jesus—
the One on whom the Spirit descended;
the One who bestowed this selfsame power,
and with his presence attended.

I need a fresh vision of Jesus—
the One who sought the lost and wounded;
the One who sincerely cared for sinners
and from their hell and night lifted.

I need a fresh vision of Jesus—
the One who stooped to wash dirty feet;
the One who didn't cling to his status,
but with joy served even the least.

I need a fresh vision of Jesus—
the One who came to do his Father's will;
the One who drank the bitter cup fully,
bearing all the shame on that Hill.

I need a fresh vision of Jesus—
the One seated at the Father's right hand;
the One bearing the wounds from Calvary,
who pleads our case when we don't stand.

I need a fresh vision of Jesus—
the One risen and now reigning above ;
the One who by his indwelling Spirit,
prepares his Bride to reign in love.

I need a fresh vision of Jesus.

Seeing Jesus

And when they lifted up their eyes, they saw no one but Jesus only.
— Matthew 17:8

The Lord Jesus can only be seen through the eyes of loving faith. Such loving faith causes his disciples to experience a heavenly and incomprehensible joy: "Though you have not seen him, you love him. Though you do not now see him, you believe in him and rejoice with joy that is inexpressible and filled with glory" (1 Pet. 1:8). But our vision of Jesus can be blurred. When this is the case, our faith becomes weak and our love grows cold. Then the joy wanes and the glory fades.

When the vision of the Lord Jesus begins to grow dim in the Christian's walk, the Holy Spirit is there to gently renew clarity, discernment, and assurance. No God-thirsty believer will be content to go a very long distance with an impaired vision of Jesus. We need the regular touches of Jesus in order to maintain a fresh vision of Jesus. Otherwise, our view of Jesus becomes distorted and we grow distant.

Do you remember the blind man that was brought to Jesus one day? Jesus led the man outside the village of Bethsaida, whereupon Jesus spat on his eyes and laid his hands on the man's eyes. Jesus asked the man what he saw. The man responded: "I see men, but they look like trees, walking." Jesus was not content to leave the man incomplete, so he touched the man's eyes once more. This time when the man opened his eyes, “he saw everything clearly” (see Mark 8:22-26).

The gaze of the disciples of Jesus is always to be directed to him: “*looking* to Jesus, the founder and perfecter of our faith . . .” (Heb. 12:2, emphasis added). This “looking” should always be the constant gaze of the soul. But what are we to do when we discover it isn’t? What are we to do when our vision of Jesus grows dim—a vision of his love, mercy, and compassion; his holiness, righteousness, and truth; his power, gentleness, courage, and perseverance? What are we to do?

This is what we are to do—let Jesus take us aside and touch us anew. Let us bow before him, waiting in his presence, being still. And stay there until we begin to see him clearly once again.

In the words of George MacDonald (1824-1905):

I waited for the Master
  In the darkness dumb;
Light came fast and faster—
  My light did not come!
I waited all the daylight,
  All through noon’s hot flame:
In the evening’s gray light,
  Lo, the Master came![30]

Rekindling the Gift

I had allowed myself to become spiritually depleted;
the pressures of ministry had drained my energy.

My natural tendency to timidity had resurfaced;
I was more in fear of man than of God.

As the Great Shepherd's under-shepherd,
I was not serving with confidence and boldness.

I was tempted to think of ministry
in terms of position, profession and prestige.

The strength to labor was weak;
my vision of Christ had grown dim.

My passionate love for Christ and people
were being threatened by lesser things.

The disciplines of godliness
were like embers with a faint glow.

Then I received a timely word
from my father in Christ:

"Timothy, rekindle the gift of God that is within you through the laying on of my hands; for God did not give us a spirit of timidity, but a spirit of power and love and self-control."

I left the house with the scroll in my hand,
seeking a quiet place, determined to rekindle the gift.

(Based on 2 Timothy 1:6-7.)

A Pastor's Daily Prayer

O God, my Father,

inasmuch as I have been chosen according to your foreknowledge, through the sanctifying work of the Holy Spirit, for obedience to Jesus Christ and sprinkling by his blood;

inasmuch as you have also predestined me to be conformed to the likeness of your Son;

inasmuch as you chose me in Christ before the creation of the world to be holy and blameless in your sight;

inasmuch as I have a Great High Priest who has ascended into Heaven, Jesus the Son of God;

inasmuch as I have been made holy through the sacrifice of the body of Jesus Christ once for all;

inasmuch as you who have called me is holy—be pleased this day to so fill me with your Spirit, that I may be empowered to will and to do all your good pleasure.

And finally, O righteous Father, when I fall short of your perfect righteousness (which I do so daily), I appeal to my Advocate at your right hand, who ever lives to make intercession for imperfect saints, that his meritorious blood may speak to you on my behalf.

Thank you, Father, for hearing this petition from your unworthy under-shepherd, who has been made worthy through the blood of your beloved Son, the Lord Jesus Christ. Amen.

Room to Grow

I thought I was dead to SELF—
until I became defensive
when told of a character weakness.

I thought I was KIND—
until I became harsh
while correcting my child.

I thought I was CONSIDERATE—
until I became thoughtless
when I failed to say "Thank you."

I thought I was PATIENT—
until I became irritated
at the driver in front of me.

I thought I was GLORIFYING God—
until I made reference
as to how God had used me.

I thought I was GUILELESS—
until I struggled to be totally honest
when updating my resume.

I thought I was COMPASSIONATE—
until I failed to visit
a sick neighbor.

I thought I was SELFLESS—
until I realized I was more generous

spending on myself than others.

I thought I had FORGIVEN all who had wronged me—
until I shared with a friend
how someone had betrayed me.

I thought I was incapable of ENVY—
until I felt uneasy toward someone else
being honored instead of me.

I thought I had no love for the things of the WORLD—
until I looked back a second time
to admire my new car.

I thought I had good MANNERS—
until I was rude
with the waitress.

I thought I was comfortable with my GIFTS—
until I began to compare mine
to another more gifted than I.

I thought I wasn't SELF-ABSORBED—
until I became more interested in telling my story
than I did in listening to his.

I thought I was GRACIOUS—
until I responded with sarcasm
and saw her countenance fall.

I thought I warmly ACCEPTED all true Christians—
until I discovered he belonged

to a different group in the body of Christ.

I thought I was CHARITABLE—
until I didn't put the best
construction on what she said.

I thought God was in CONTROL of me—
until I tried
to control my spouse.

I thought I was a WITNESS for Christ—
until I shrank from sharing the gospel
with a needy sinner.

I thought my GROWTH was satisfactory—
until I knelt again today before the Cross
and looked up into the face of Christ.

Prayer:
O Christ of God, let me never imagine that I can for one moment
live a Christlike life without your constant abiding presence.
Without you I am nothing; without you I can do nothing.
I can only overcome every foe as I continually gaze upon you.
Strengthen me, I pray, by your ever-present, indwelling Spirit.
Amen.

The Desert

God led you into a desert
to test you once again.
The place appears dry and barren,
not beautiful for man.

"Why am I here?" you ask with tears.
He chooses not to say.
You need not to know the reason;
look up to him and stay.

"There's no glory in the desert;
this place I don't deserve.
All's still and very silent here,
what purpose can it serve?"

Be faithful in the desert place,
holding forth faith's strong shield;
Don't hasten soon to go your way,
until your all you yield.

Drink deeply in the desert;
be refreshed and renewed.
Let his Spirit fill you fully,
then go forth and be used.

Deepened by Deserts

. . . for I give water in the wilderness, rivers in the desert . . .
— Isaiah 43:20

Deserts are neither for novices nor tourists. Deserts are for maturing saints.

A desert is a place—both geographically and spiritually—which is basically barren. It is a region with very little or no rainfall. The vegetation, if any, is sparse and rarely does one see any species deserving of the name *tree.*

Deserts are usually uninhabited. *Normal* people don't choose to live in deserts, unless of course, there is a ready supply of air conditioning by day and heat by night. Deserts can be tough—tough on bodies, tough on souls.

While there were men who came to be known as "Desert Fathers," who in the fourth century chose geographically arid regions of Egypt, Palestine and Syria to isolate themselves from the general population in order to concentrate completely on God, no Christian would choose a "dry place" as a place to stimulate spiritual fruitfulness. Yet God chooses to lead his thirsted-hearted saints periodically to travel into desert places—not to break them, but to *make* them.

Deserts are meant not for talking. Deserts are quite places, places meant for listening—listening to God.

Deserts are not made for harvests; harvests are for another season. Deserts are meant to destroy—destroy our dependencies on *things*, our *toys*, our *sovereign selves*.

Deserts are one of God's favorite and most effective instruments of mercy in producing in us his holiness and wholeness, his symmetry and beauty. We are cleansed in the desert—cleansed of impurities, cleansed of self-delusions, cleansed of unrealities. The desert is intended to make us real, authentic, genuine. The Holy Spirit burns intensely in the desert.

It was in a desert that Moses heard God's call.

The Spirit led Jesus into a desert.

Deserts inevitably precede fruitfulness.

Don't resist the deserts. Embrace them. In time you will learn to bless God for them.

God cannot make saints without deserts. Don't search for a substitute. There is none.

Whose Glory?

Showmanship or discipleship—
which one will it be:
Parading our flesh of success,
or walking humbly?

The lofty looks, the boastful claims,
punctuate our days;
Little souls are rewarded by
man's flattering praise.

The need to be seen, to be first,
controls every plan;
Impressions are all-important,
applause fuels the man.

To draw attention to ourselves,
bragging of our deeds,
To angle for the praise of men
is wood, straw and weeds.

Lights, we are, to shine before men—
our good works to see;
Not that we should be glorified,
but his Majesty.

Let's be disciples of the Lord,
gazing on the Lamb;
Humbly walking in his footprints,
rejecting the sham.

The Speaking Word

Showmanship or discipleship . . .

God opposes the proud, but gives grace to the humble.

— James 4:6

The lofty looks, the boastful claims . . .

One's pride will bring him low, but he who is lowly in spirit will obtain honor.

— Proverbs 29:23

The need to be seen, to be first . . .

And he sat down and called the twelve. And he said to them, "If anyone would be first, he must be last of all and servant of all."

— Mark 9:35

To draw attention to ourselves . . .

. . . the LORD declares: "Far be it from me, for those who honor me I will honor, and those who despise me shall be lightly esteemed."

— 1 Samuel 2:30

Lights, we are, to shine before men . . .

". . . let your light shine before others, so that they may see your good works and give glory to your Father who is in heaven."

— Matthew 5:16

Lord, What About This Man?

How God chooses to lead others
is not for me to question;
For he is the sovereign Lord
and leads by his own discretion.
It is not for me to ask,
"Lord, what about this man?"

Spirit-gifts and fields of service
have been carefully assigned,
To each of his own children
by a Father who's good and kind.
It is not for me to ask,
"Lord, what about this man?"

If for me the path he's chosen
may seem difficult and hard,
I'm glancing at my brothers
instead of gazing on the Lord.
It is not for me to ask,
"Lord, what about this man?"

God has called none of his children
to quiz him on these matters;
But to only follow Christ,
trusting him to guide our brothers.
It is not for me to ask,
"Lord, what about this man?"

(Based on John 21:20-23.)

Glancing Over Our Shoulder

[21]When Peter saw him, he said to Jesus, "Lord, what about this man?" [22]Jesus said to him, "If it is my will that he remain until I come, what is that to you? You follow me!" [23]So the saying spread abroad among the brothers that this disciple was not to die; yet Jesus did not say to him that he was not to die, but, "If it is my will that he remain until I come, what is that to you?"
— John 21:21-23

There is a temptation which we have all yielded to at one time or another—the temptation to compare ourselves or our ministry to another brother or sister in Christ or to another ministry. This is always self-defeating.

Some time ago I was perusing an excellent Christian periodical that had come across my desk. I noticed in the credits section that the magazine had a circulation of over 40,000 subscribers. Although this paper has been in circulation for over 40 years and is sent free to its readership, nevertheless, almost involuntarily I began to wonder why it would have such a larger readership than *Life in the Spirit* journal. I had no more begun to make such a comparison, when the Spirit led me to the above passage. And while meditating on Christ's rejoinder to Peter, the words of the following poem came to mind.

Dipping his pen into the inkwell of divine inspiration, the Apostle Paul wrote that those who compare themselves among themselves are not wise (see 2 Cor. 10:12). How is that so? Why is it unwise to make comparisons in the family of God? It is unwise to make comparisons among ourselves and our respective ministries because . . .

▪ *Our gifts differ*. The Spirit distributes gifts in the church according to his sovereign will. Moses is not to be compared with Elijah; neither is Paul to be compared with Timothy. God gives different gifts in order to build a balanced church.

▪ *Our callings differ*. Some are called to leadership roles, others to supportive ministries. Some have one unique gift to share with the Body of Christ, others are multi-gifted.

▪ *It can make us envious*. If we are comparing our gifts to one we perceive to be more gifted, it can cause us to inwardly wish we had the same gift.

▪ *It can create discontent*. To accept and be content with the gifts we have been given by God is a beautiful thing. Otherwise, we are questioning the goodness and wisdom of God.

▪ *It can make us proud*. If we compare our gifts to those we perceive as having inferior gifts, it can only foster pride.

Let us ask God to help us not look over our shoulder. Instead, let us keep our eyes fixed on Jesus.

Pleasing the Lord

To live my life to please the Master
Should be my controlling ambition;
Regardless of my circumstances,
Pleasing Christ should be my sole passion.

Whatever my status or calling,
Wherever Providence has placed me—
The Lord's grace is more than sufficient
To strengthen my heart for the journey.

Am I afflicted or much oppressed?
Am I tempted to lose heart and zest?
Will I falter in running this race?
Or will I trust Christ in this sore test?

My skilled Adversary, on the prowl,
Is roaring like a hungry lion;
He stalks those who are wounded the most,
And pounces when ripe our condition.

If I should fail in pleasing the Lord,
The Spirit will be put to some grief;
Like a dove when offended and hurt,
He takes his flight till given relief.

Since it brings great joy to God's own heart
When his dear children choose to please him,
The shield of faith I'll hold, by his grace,
Until the Day I rise to meet him.

Moral Acuity

. . . try to discern what is pleasing to the Lord.
— Ephesians 5:10

Because one's moral acuity is a major factor in spiritual integrity and maturity, it is critical to the Christian's growth that he is always learning what brings great pleasure to the heart of his God. The apostle Paul knew this, thus he writes to the Ephesian believers: "try to discern what is pleasing to the Lord" (Eph. 5:10).

This apostolic admonition was directed toward those who had been converted to Christ out of rank paganism, and who lived in a society which lacked a moral compass. While our particular conversion environment may have differed from that of these Ephesians, the moral climate each of us lives in is not far removed from theirs, thus the need for moral discernment.

How does the Christian develop moral acuity (i.e., the ability to perceive what pleases the Lord when faced with moral decisions)? Let's look at the immediate context of Ephesians 5 for our answers.

- *Walk in love* (v.1). It is only as we are continually filled with *agape* love for God and other people that we are prepared to make moral judgments. How can one be filled with the love of God and be angry, bitter, and unforgiving toward his brothers and sisters in Christ (see Eph. 4:31-32)?

▪ *Stay clear of impurity* (vv. 3, 5). We live in a dirty age. Many Christians are even being told from some pulpits that sexual purity is an ideal that cannot be realized in this world—that it is normal (even for a Christian) to lust, etc. Is it any wonder that so many Christians are living defeated lives? Paul says there is a certain kind of sexual behavior that is expected of saints—true believers.

▪ *Guard your tongue* (v. 4). Profanity, obscenity, and vulgarity have no place in the language of Christians; off-colored jokes are totally unbecoming. Rather, let the tongue be employed in expressions of thanks.

▪ *Walk as children of light* (vv. 8-17). One cannot exercise keen moral judgment while walking in darkness. We are to walk in the light—the truth—of God.

▪ *Be always filled with the Spirit.* (vv. 18-21). To be filled with the Spirit is to live under the Spirit's control. As we live under the Spirit's control, the Spirit sharpens our moral acuity, which in turn brings great pleasure to the heart of our Father in Heaven.

Be assured, God provides moral discernment to those who seriously seek it . . . and are living on the necessary spiritual plane to receive it.

Lest We Drift

[1]Therefore we must pay much closer attention to what we have heard, lest we drift away from it. [2]For since the message declared by angels proved to be reliable, and every transgression or disobedience received a just retribution, [3]how shall we escape if we neglect such a great salvation?
— Hebrews 2:1-3

To listen very carefully
to the truth we have heard,
Is a message from the Spirit
sent to us from God's Word.

Like a ship without a rudder
or a vessel without sail,
Is a Christian who does not act
on the truth without fail.

The message given through angels
always proved to be true;
Transgressors were justly punished,
exceptions were but few.

What makes us think we can escape
God's punishment for sin,
If we respond indifferently
to the Lord's salvation?

Awake, Christian! Pay attention!
lest the truth of God you neglect.
The storm is raging all around;
be careful lest you drift!

Am I a Soldier of the Cross?

Be watchful, stand firm in the faith, act like men, be strong.
— 1 Corinthians 16:13

The Christian is called to be a valiant soldier for the Lord Jesus Christ. From the moment of conversion onward, the disciple of Christ is engaged in warfare against the world, the flesh, and the Devil. This is no pilgrimage for the faint of heart.

One of the Church's greatest hymn writers was Isaac Watts (1674-1748); he was also a pastor. He once preached a sermon from 1 Corinthians 16:13, a text filled with militant terminology. In that text Paul challenges the Corinthian believers: "Be watchful, stand firm in the faith, act like men, be strong." In preparation to preach his sermon, Watts composed a hymn titled "Am I a Soldier of the Cross?"

In the hymn, Watts asks the congregation to seriously consider a series of searching questions. The first question addresses the matter of living as a witness for Christ before a watching world.

Am I a soldier of the cross,
A follower of the Lamb,
And shall I fear to own His cause,
Or blush to speak His Name?

The second question addresses the subject of total consecration.

Must I be carried to the skies
On flowery beds of ease,
While others fought to win the prize,
And sailed through bloody seas?

The next series of questions consider our response to a hostile world.

Are there no foes for me to face?
Must I not stem the flood?
Is this vile world a friend to grace,
To help me on to God?

What was the pastor/hymn writer's answer?

Sure I must fight if I would reign;
Increase my courage, Lord.
I'll bear the toil, endure the pain,
Supported by Thy Word.[31]

In the strength of the Spirit, let every disciple of Christ offer a resounding "Amen!" to the challenge of this classic hymn writer.

A True Brother

I labored with a heavy load,
filled with anxiety and care;
My shoulders sagged, as did my soul,
the burden was too great to bear.

Afar, a brother watched my struggle,
making no effort to come near;
Shouting instead, "Cheer up, fella,
the day is all sunny and clear."

I stumbled on, doing my best,
the end of the road to make;
Wanting to be strong in this test,
lest under my great load I break.

Then I felt another at my side;
he placed his hand gently on me.
Not an empty word did he speak;
and his tears flowed warmly and free.

I began to regain lost strength,
the hour I felt my brother's hand;
And saw the tears flow from his eyes—
convinced that he did understand.

Friendship

A friend loves at all times,
and a brother is born for adversity.
— Proverbs 17:17

Authentic Christian friends are a gift from God and by the very nature and demands of friendship, they are few. Because we are a part of the family of God, everyone who is in Christ is our brother or sister, but not necessarily a close friend.

None of us has many friends, and that's the way it should be. We have a host of acquaintances and contacts, but only a few friends. Why is this so? Because genuine friendship requires compatibility, flexibility, availability, and unconditional acceptance.

Compatibility. Just as a couple in a healthy marriage, genuine friends are compatible. They are not "carbon copies" of one another, but they have the ability to relate to each other with a high degree of harmony. Their dissimilarities don't get in the way of a growing, loving relationship.

Flexibility. True friends give each other space; they are not demanding; they don't force themselves on each another. One cannot be possessive and develop a true friendship.

Availability. Genuine friendships require time. It takes time to grow a friendship, and it takes time to maintain a friendship.

Friends want to be with each other. There are some relationships which could blossom into beautiful friendships, if the two parties would simply take the time to invest in each other. Of course, it takes two. One person can't be the one always initiating the contact.

Unconditional acceptance. Authentic friends are non-judgmental. One can be totally transparent with a friend without fear of endangering the friendship. Candor is one of friendship's traits. Friends don't wear masks.

We all need friends. I pray that you are blessed, as I am, with a few genuine Christian friends.

Prayer: *Father, I thank you for my friends. Grant me the necessary sensitivity and wisdom to be a true friend to all of my friends. Amen.*

Affirmation

I have just received affirmation
for some small duties I had done;
Gracious words were sincerely spoken
profusely—one right after one.

The thoughtfulness of every person
with gratitude has been received;
They took the time for commendation,
the load I carried they relieved.

Select words, spoken in due season,
comes to the soul like a sweet balm;
In a world that's full of commotion,
kind words can produce a great calm.

And, yet, I must not keep all this praise,
though given with best intention;
For I know Who has ordered my ways—
He's deserving of all attention.

What shall I do when I'm thus honored,
knowing the credit I can't take?
Here's what I will do when men applaud:
to Christ all the kind words I'll take!

An Encouraging Word

Anxiety in a man's heart weighs him down,
but a good word makes him glad.
— Proverbs 12:25

To make an apt answer is a joy to a man,
and a word in season, how good it is!
— Proverbs 15:23

Gracious words are like a honeycomb,
sweetness to the soul and health to the body.
— Proverbs 16:24

As a little boy, while attending elementary school, I well remember a song our chorus teacher taught us one day. It's a western ballad that most American school children used to learn at one time or another—"Home On the Range." There is a line in this song that should serve as a standard of speech for all Christians: "And never was heard a discouraging word."

Words—how powerful they are; how motivating and inspirational they can be. Impressionable words, spoken by a significant person, can even chart the course for the rest of one's life.

Benjamin West (1738-1820) tells how he became a great artist. One day his mother left the house, leaving young Benjamin in charge of his little sister Sally. In his mother's absence, Benjamin discovered some bottles of colored ink and decided to try and paint a portrait of his sister. But in doing so, he made quite a mess of things and ink blots ended up all over the room.

After some time, his mother returned. She quickly surveyed the mess, but said nothing. She picked up the piece of paper and saw Benjamin's drawing. "Why," she exclaimed, "It's Sally!" And she stooped to kiss her son. Ever afterward, Benjamin West used to say, "My mother's words and kiss made me a painter."

While a Christian will avoid flattery—insincere complimentary words—he will search out ways in which he can bring comfort and encouragement, inspiration and affirmation, to God's dear children.

After receiving several affirming comments from my students at the conclusion of a New Testament course I taught in a local university, I wrote the previous poem, I hope can be used by our gracious Lord to encourage you, dear reader.

Let it be said of us: "And never was heard a discouraging word!"

Prayer for Bible Reading/Study

O God, my Father, I am about to open the pages of your written revelation—your holy Word.

I humbly confess my inherent lack of wisdom and understanding; my natural dullness to spiritual verities; my tendency to cold-heartedness and indifference. If I am to grow in the grace and knowledge of the Lord Jesus Christ, I must hear your voice and see your ways. I plead: Send your Holy Spirit to make this a meaningful time of worship and learning.

Because I am naturally ignorant of the ways of your truth and righteousness—instruct me in your knowledge and wisdom.

Because I tend to err and am easily inclined to follow my own ways—correct my false impressions and the delusions of my own thinking.

Because of my background, prejudices and fallen nature, I am inclined to interpret your Word according to my own biases; guard my heart and mind by your Spirit. May I bow to only your truth, not man-made caricatures.

Because when I have failed you, I am inclined to live in the shadows instead of walking in your light, convict me, I pray, of my sins; and open my eyes to your holiness, love and forgiveness.

Because I realize it is possible to deceive myself into thinking that the reading of your Word is the equivalent of obeying your Word, keep me from this grave deception.

Be pleased to supply me with the necessary grace required to apply your commands, principles and teachings to every area of my life.

Grant, O Father, that through the reading and study of your holy Word that I will worship you more fully, love you more dearly, and follow you more nearly.

As you renew my mind through meditating upon your Word today, empower me as I go out into the world to discern the real from the false, truth from error.

O righteous Father, according to your infinite wisdom, knowledge and love, use your Word in me as a hammer . . . use your Word as balm . . . use your Word as fire . . . use your Word as light . . but please, O Lord, accomplish your eternal purposes in me through your gracious Word.

Thank you, Father, for answering this petition, offered by your unworthy servant, in the name of my Mediator, Jesus Christ the Lord. Amen.

Christ's Commands

Some years ago I did a personal Bible study on the commands of Christ for my own edification. During that study I marked the margin of my Bible with a red "c" for each of our Lord's respective commands, as recorded in the four Gospels. With the exception of the "Leadership" heading, to the best of my knowledge the following commands are considered by our Lord to be universally applicable for all Christians for all time.

Why should these commands receive our serious attention? Consider the following words of our Lord:

"If you love me, you will keep my commandments" (John 14:15, NASB);

"Whoever who has my commandments and keeps them, he it is who loves Me" (John 14:21, NASB);

"If you keep my commandments, you will abide in My love . . ." (John 15:10, NASB).

May the love of God the Father, the grace of the Lord Jesus Christ, and the sanctifying ministry of the Holy Spirit accompany you as you seek to personally apply the following commands to your own life.

Note: Where commands are repeated in the Gospels, I have listed the first occurrence. Also, I have created subject headings for those wishing to do a topical study.

Grandchildren

[14]But as for you, continue in what you have learned and have firmly believed, knowing from whom you learned it [15]and how from childhood you have been acquainted with the sacred writings, which are able to make you wise for salvation through faith in Christ Jesus.
— 2 Timothy 3:14-15

Every earnest Christian desires that one's children and children's children will grow up to serve the Lord Jesus Christ. Emily and I are blessed to have two lovely daughters, who have served Christ from their childhood. We fervently pray that our three precious grandchildren—Luke (eight years of age), Emily and Jacob (twins, six years of age) will do the same.

On my last pastorate, Luke would occasionally attend the mid-week prayer service with Emily and me. As I stood in front, opening the service with prayer, he would spontaneously slip to my side (at 3 and 4 years of age), and repeat my prayer after me. Like Samuel as a child, he has a sensitivity to the Lord. We pray the same for Emily and Jacob.

The following poem was written when Luke was three years old. As the author, I placed the words vicariously into his mouth, praying for him. Since then, we often pray together.

Let me encourage you, dear reader, if you have children and grandchildren, to keep them covered with your fervent, believing prayers.

Luke's Prayer

Dear Jesus, though very little,
I want you to live in my heart,
And teach me how to love others,
and to love you—doing my part.

I want to be good, Dear Jesus—
to make Mommy and Daddy proud.
Help me to be real good today,
not to act naughty and be loud.

Help me to obey my parents,
when they tell me what to do—
To be nice to Jack and Jacob,
to be kind to Emily, too.

Thank you, Dear Jesus, for my tools—
my blower and my weedwacker.
I thank you, too, for all my balls,
my shovel, and Daddy's tractor.

I'm just little now, Dear Jesus;
some day I'm gonna be bigger.
Boys will ask me to do bad things;
please protect me from the Tempter.

And when I grow up to be big,
let me not from you ever stray;
But always serve you, Dear Jesus,
until you take me Home some day.

My Mother

It gives me great pleasure to include in this volume the following poem written by my dear mother, who went to be with the Lord in December 1956, shortly after I had turned twelve years of age.

All who knew Ruth Tilley knew her to be a praying woman, full of good works. I recently re-read two years of her daily diaries (1953 and 1954); they are punctuated again and again with praises to her Lord and intercessions for her family and friends. She fell asleep in Jesus while on her knees. My godly mother is now with Christ, but her prayers remain before the Throne and are still being answered.

It is because of our merciful Lord's graciously working through our mother's life and prayers, that one by one her five children entered the Kingdom of God. Her two sons (Gordon and Ralph) have served Christ and his church in a variety of responsibilities—pastor, professor, denominational official, editor, publisher, evangelist, and writer. One daughter (Mary) has served as a pastor's wife for many years, and the other two daughters (Sharon and Dorothy) have actively served their respective churches in a variety of responsible ways.

The following poem provides only a small glimpse into the kind of praying and caring person Ruth Tilley was—in her home, neighborhood, and church. "Her children rise up and call her blessed" (Prov. 31:2).

Neighbors

by Leona Ruth Tilley

As I went to church this morning,
Down the old familiar street,
Past the houses of the neighbors,
All well kept and very neat,
How our heart leaps up within us
As we think upon each one;
How we hope again to meet them
When we've passed Life's Setting Sun.

There's the Frankes and the Morrows,
Very close to us live they;
How it cheers our heart to hear them say,
"Good Morning," Mrs. Tilley."
Then across the street a little way,
The Huffmans do reside—
It's Ivory and Gladys,
And Bob close by their side.

We are so slow of speech it seems,
We never can relate
How much their presence means to us,
For when we pass their gate—
If they are anywhere around
In sight as we go by—
They always greet us cheerily,
"Good Morning," or just, "Hi."

Then on the other side of Bob
Is the Ritzes' dwelling place;
There we find Mr. & Mrs. Ritz,
Lois, and Jimmy's smiling face.
They always have a word so kind
To say as we pass on;

And we have learned to love them all,
We hate not "nary" one.

We couldn't forget the Pattengills,
Who live on Cleveland Street;
It's just the second door from us
In a little house, so neat.
How often as we rush outside,
With a pan, or maybe two,
They never fail to greet us,
"Good evening," or, "How are you?"

Then on beyond the Pattengills,
The Edwards; they reside
In a little house of brick coating,
And very neat inside.
And in the summertime her flowers
Are all in stately rows;
She spends much time among them
And each variety she knows.

Then by the side of Ritzes
The Mingous Boys dwell,
And Mrs. Richey, Audrey and girls—
Their names are hard to spell.
Little Nyoka and Needra,
How sweet they are to see;
And as they pass our house,
How happy they seem to be.

Then on the other side of them—
Together, the Query Four—
And as I pass by her sometimes
She greets me from her door.
On beyond the Query's dwelling,
At six hundred thirty-nine,
Live the Greens—Gladys and Carolyn

These people are so fine.
How our heart does move with pity,
As we think upon their son,
Who gave his life in Korea,
Ere the battle had been won.

Then as we move along, you know,
There's the Battins at 647—
Jimmy, Johnny, with Mr. and Mrs.—
How we hope we can meet in Heaven.
Across from them, another family
By the name of Green—
Arthur and Mary—are also here,
Their faces we've often seen.

Upon the very corner
As we turn on Ohio—
The Dulongs live together—
Their faces we've learned to know.
She always seems so friendly,
And the children, we love them all;
We pray there won't be one missing,
Dear Lord, at your last Roll Call.

"Kitty-cornered" across from them—
Live McIntoshs, Rosie and Herb
Janice, and Larry McIntosh—
Behind a decorated curb.
Then on the south side of us
Is where Mrs. Snyder lives—
A piano teacher of some note—
And many lessons she gives.

Across from Mrs. Snyder,
The Cook's house we can see—
Mr. and Mrs. Sherman Cook
Make up this family.

Next door north of Sherman Cook
Is Mrs. Settles's abode;
We can see it plainly from our house—
"Kitty-cornered" across the road.

Now as we close our little poem,
We wish to utter a prayer:
"Dear Lord, we pray that we may meet
Them—every one up there—
And not a single one will miss
That home thou hast gone to prepare—
The pearly gates and golden streets
Of that city, oh, so fair."

How it will pay us everyone
To strive to enter in,
To lay aside the tattered garments
All spotted and stained with sin.
And in exchange receive a robe,
All dazzling, spotless, and white;
For only such may enter in
That city, oh, so bright.

Our blessed Lord has paid the price;
We need not miss the way.
He bore our sins upon the cross;
His life for us down he did lay.
So now we want to say, "Adieu,
God bless you, everyone!
We hope to see each one of you,
When our earthly race is run."

Renewing My Covenant

O God, my Father, today I rejoice in your fellowship. What more could one desire than to know you, the only true God, and Jesus Christ whom you have sent?

> *"Oh, the depth of the riches of the wisdom and knowledge of God! How unsearchable are his judgments, and how inscrutable his ways!"*[32]

Father, my spirit craves your fellowship! More than food and drink, more than earthly companionship, more than life itself, I desire to walk hand in hand, heart to heart with you.

> *I Love Thee so, I know not how*
> *My transports to control;*
> *Thy love is like a burning fire*
> *Within my very soul.*[33]

O Christ, you said:

> *"If anyone loves me, he will keep my word, and my Father will love him, and we will come to him and make our home with him."*[34]

This very day, I renew my covenant with you. By the grace you supply—I would obey your teachings; I would gladly embrace your commands. For I want you, and the Father, and the blessed Holy Spirit to be at home in your temple, my body.

Grant me, O my Lord, the unremitting desire and strength to moment-by-moment walk in fellowship with you. May I shun every known sin like the plague; may I flee every enemy of the Cross; may my desires be only for you.

O righteous Father, forgive me for every instance in which my love for you was diminished, and for those occasions when I desired something more than I desired you. O Father, in the name of your Son, I pray that you will cover those failures by the blood of your Son.

In the strong name of the Lord Jesus Christ, who is my Lord and Savior, I offer this petition. Amen.

Praying for My Readers

To each reader of this volume—both known and unknown to me:

Because the Lord brought you to my mind today,
I lifted up my heart and for you did pray;
What a wonderful token his love bestows,
When he brings to our minds the children he chose.

Notes

1. Taken from "And Can It Be?" by Charles Wesley.
2. Taken from "O for a Thousand Tongues to Sing" by Charles Wesley.
3. Cited by Andrew Bonar, *The Life of Robert Murray M'Cheyne* (London: The Banner of Truth Trust, 1844; reprinted 1962) 185.
4. Taken from "Oh, to Be Like Thee" by Thomas O. Chisholm.
5. A. W. Tozer, *The Pursuit of God* (Harrisburg, PA: Christian Publications, 1948) 15.
6. Taken from "Arise, My Soul Arise" by Charles Wesley.
7. C. F. Keil and F. Delitzsch, *Commentary on the Old Testament,* vol. 1 (Grand Rapids, MI: Wm. B. Eerdmans, 1981, reprint) 136.
8. J. I. Packer, *Knowing God* (Downers Grove, IL: InterVarsity Press, 1973) 20.
9. Wayne Grudem, *Systematic Theology* (Grand Rapids, MI: Zondervan, 1994) 149.
10. I have been unable to locate the primary source for this quotation. Some speculate the conversation between Wesley and Oglethorpe is a myth; if it is, the narrative remains true just the same.
11. A. W. Tozer, *The Knowledge of the Holy* (New York: Harper & Brothers Publishers, 1961) 10.
12. Adam Clarke, *Clarke's Commentary*, vol. 1 (Nashville, TN: Abingdon Press, reprint, n. d.) 27.
13. Taken from "Am I a Soldier of the Cross?" by Isaac Watts.
14. The primary source for this quotation is unknown to me.
15. C. S. Lewis, *Mere Christianity* (New York: Macmillan Publishing Co., 1952) 140.
16. Cited by Thomas Cook, *New Testament Holiness* (London: The Epworth Press, 1958) 6.
17. Karl Menninger, *Whatever Became of Sin?* (New York: Hawthorn Books, 1973) 17.
18. J. Sidlow Baxter, *Going Deeper* (Grand Rapids, MI: Zondervan, 1959) 133-134.
19. Taken from "Take Time to Be Holy" by William D. Longstaff.
20. Charles G. Finney, *Charles G. Finney: An Autobiography* (Old Tappan, NJ: Fleming H. Revell Co., 1908) 10.
21. Fred A. Hartley, *Everything by Prayer: Armin Gesswein's Keys to Spirit-Filled Living* (Camp Hill, PA: Christian Publications, 2003) 36.
22. Tozer, *The Pursuit of God,* 15.

23. Taken from “Jesus, Thou Joy of Loving Hearts” by Bernard of Clairvaux.
24. Søren Kierkegaard, *Purity of Heart is to Will One Thing* (New York: Harper & Row, 1948) 209-210.
25. Lewis, *Mere Christianity*, 111.
26. Downloaded October 2005 from Iowa State University’s Horticulture & Home Pest News website: http://www.ipm.iastate.edu/ipm/hortnews/1995/3-3-1995/prune.htm.
27. Duncan Campbell, *Duncan Campbell: The Story of a Soul Winner* (Hobe Sound, FL: H.S.B.C. Press, n.d.) 6.
28. Taken from “All for Jesus” by Mary D. James.
29. George MacDonald, *Knowing the Heart of God*, edited by Michael R. Phillips (Minneapolis, MN: Bethany House Publishers, 1990) 253.
30. Ibid., 97.
31. Taken from “Am I a Soldier of the Cross?” by Isaac Watts.
32. Romans 11:33.
33. Taken from “O Jesus, Jesus, Dearest Lord!” by Frederick W. Faber.
34. John 14:23.

About
Life in the Spirit Ministries

Life in the Spirit Ministries was founded in 1993 and publishes ***Life in the Spirit*** journal, a 40-page bimonthly publication consisting of articles on the themes of spiritual renewal and formation; both classic and current authors appear in the journal. This ministry also serves the Christian public through the Internet and publishes a select number of books and pamphlets.

Life in the Spirit Ministries, Inc. is registered with the United States of America Internal Revenue Service as a 501 (c) (3) not-for-profit corporation.

To receive a free trial issue of ***Life in the Spirit*** journal or for more information, you may contact us at one of the following addresses:

editor@litsjournal.org

www.litsjournal.org

Life in the Spirit
P.O. Box 405
Sellersburg, Indiana 47172

www.ingramcontent.com/pod-product-compliance
Lightning Source LLC
Chambersburg PA
CBHW032116040426
42449CB00005B/167